DIVINE MARRIAGE

DIVINE MARRIAGE

Discovering the Blessing and Beauty of a Covenant Relationship

LUIS & KRISTEN ROMÁN

*Divine Marriage: Discovering the Blessing
and Beauty of a Covenant Relationship*
Copyright © 2021 by Luis & Kristen Roman

Printed by XO Latino, a division of XO Marriage and XO Publishing

This book, or parts thereof, may not be reproduced in any form or by any means without written permission from the publisher, except brief passages for purposes of reviews. For information, contact XO Marriage™.

P.O Box 59888
Dallas, Texas 75229
1-800-380-6330
Or visit our website at xomarriage.com

XO Publishing

All Scripture quotations, unless otherwise indicated, are taken from the Holy Bible, New International Version®, NIV®. Copyright ©1973, 1978, 1984, 2011 by Biblica, Inc.™ Used by permission of Zondervan. All rights reserved worldwide. www.zondervan.com. The "NIV" and "New International Version" are trademarks registered in the United States Patent and Trademark Office by Biblica, Inc.™

Scripture quotations marked (KJV) are taken from the King James Version. Public domain.

Scripture quotations marked (NKJV) are taken from the New King James Version®. Copyright © 1982 by Thomas Nelson. Used by permission. All rights reserved.

Scripture quotations marked (NLT) are taken from the Holy Bible, New Living Translation, copyright © 1996, 2004, 2015 by Tyndale House Foundation. Used by permission of Tyndale House Publishers, a Division of Tyndale House Ministries, Carol Stream, Illinois 60188. All rights reserved.

All rights reserved. No portion of this book may be reproduced, stored in any retrieval system, or transmitted in any form or by any means—electronic, mechanical, photocopying, recording or any other—without prior permission from the publisher.

ISBN: 978-1-950113-71-2 (Paperback)
ISBN: 978-1-950113-72-9 (eBook)

XO Publishing has no responsibility for the persistence or accuracy of URLs for external or third-party Internet websites referred to in this publication and does not guarantee that any content on such websites is or will remain accurate or appropriate.

Printed in the United States of America

Table of Contents

INTRODUCTION 1

    Chapter 1:   Covenant Foundations. 5

    Chapter 2:   Enemies of Peace .21

    Chapter 3:   Our Differences Are Our Strengths. 37

    Chapter 4:   The Secret to Intimacy. 53

    Chapter 5:   Communication Keys 75

    Chapter 6:   Conflict Resolution. 91

    Chapter 7:   Money Matters 101

    Chapter 8:   Parenting Principles 133

    Chapter 9:   New Beginnings—Blended Families. 147

CONCLUSION. 161

Introduction

IN THE FIRST YEARS OF OUR LIFE TOGETHER, we never imagined that one day we would write a book to help marriages. I (Kristen) remember perfectly the night I went downstairs to the family room with our baby in my arms. He awoke crying, frightened by our angry shouting. I tried to comfort him, rocking him and whispering promises in his ear that everything would be okay. But the truth was that I didn't believe things were going to be okay. I had lost hope, and for the first time I thought the unimaginable: *I'm leaving*. I knew I loved Luis deeply, but living together was one conflict after another, and we were emotionally exhausted. We couldn't agree on anything.

Each disagreement turned into a fiery argument, fueled by offense and pain. Now our son was paying the price, and that was the last straw. *I'm leaving.* My mind started racing in a thousand directions. *Where would I go? What would I say? God, where are You?* In that moment of despair, something supernatural happened. I heard a dog barking fiercely outside the window. That may not seem supernatural, but the window did not face the street. A high wall enclosed our yard, and our own little dog was asleep at my feet. The loud noise startled me and shook me from my frantic thoughts. In that instant a Scripture flashed through my mind: "Be alert and of sober mind. Your enemy the devil prowls around like a roaring lion looking for someone to devour" (1 Peter 5:8).

I experienced a moment of clarity, as if a veil was removed from my eyes. I understood Luis was not the enemy, and I did not have to run away from him. This was a diabolical plan to devour us and destroy God's plans in our life. Suddenly, I knew the best thing I could do for my marriage and my son was to stay and fight the enemy and not my husband. I took authority over my thoughts and began to pray fervently, binding the power of the enemy in our marriage and declaring God's purposes for our family. Things did not change overnight, but little by little we took steps towards restoration. The impact of what I experienced that night changed the course of our lives. I learned how important it is to have spiritual revelation. Jesus tells us in John 10:10, "The thief comes only to steal, kill and destroy; I have come so that they may have life, and have it to the full." The good news is in the midst of the battle, God promises abundance. That abundance is connected to the presence of Jesus. We cannot achieve this apart from Him; we need His divine touch.

The word *divine* can be defined two ways:

1. Something that comes from God (everything that comes from God expresses His characteristics)

2. Something that is noted for its beauty and positive qualities

We all want a marriage like that! One that is blessed with God's divine touch and marked by the beauty of experiencing His goodness together.

However, merely knowing what we want is not enough to make it happen. We need to know the *why* (that motivates us to change) and the *how* (that gives us the tools to make it happen). And that's the reason we decided to write this book. We have found that the key to success in marriage is understanding why God's covenant design is so important and how to practically live in the covenant blessing by applying God's promises to your relationship. We want to share what we have learned through years of ministering to couples and what we have put into practice in our own marriage. These are the same keys of success that saved us from failure in the beginning of our marriage 29 years ago. We can tell you with certainty that a successful marriage does exist. It is not perfect, but it is divine. God has given specific principles in His Word to help us develop a marriage according to His heart. If you and your spouse apply these principles, we are certain you will see God's promises and purposes fulfilled in your lives, and your marriage will be better than you ever imagined—a divine masterpiece in the making!

CHAPTER 1
Covenant **Foundations**

*In the beginning God created the heavens
and the earth.... So God created mankind in his
own image, in the image of God he created them;
male and female he created them.*
—Genesis 1:1, 27

IN THE BEGINNING, GOD CREATED ... MARRIAGE. The Creator of heaven and earth designed the perfect entity to showcase the maximum expression of His love: the union of a man and a woman created in His image. Marriage is not a man-made creation. It is made by God's design, and that's what makes it divine. The question is, if God is so great and His design so perfect, then why aren't there more marriages experiencing that divine touch? Why aren't there more marriages living in His peace and joy, showcasing His love for the world? The answer for so many is that God's presence is not the foundation of their union. **Marriage is divine only when God is in it.** When the presence of God is absent and not the anchor, marriage is simply a verbal or contractual commitment. It becomes selfish and based on false expectations of what one hopes to receive from the other person. "I got married thinking you would make me happy. I thought our marriage would be more fulfilling." It is not enough to have good intentions, ideas, goals, etc. Obviously, those things help, but a divine marriage in the biblical context has God at its foundation. Since God is the Creator of marriage, He is the only One qualified to tell us how it should work. God is supernatural, and so is a divine marriage. That is why being married under His divine blessing is not the same thing as simply joining our lives together.

Couples join their lives in one of the following ways:

- Cohabitation
- Contractual Marriage
- Covenant Marriage

You can cohabitate outside of marriage, have a contractual marriage, or have a divine covenant marriage. We are going to look beyond the obvious differences of each option to see why it is so important to understand the impact of how we are living our relationship as a couple. We hope that what we share here will be revealing and inspiring so that you can identify, "This is where we are now, but that's where we want to go, and with God's help anything is possible!"

Cohabitation

Why get married at all? People don't use the term "cohabitation" very often, but it is a relationship outside of marriage in which two people decide to join their lives by living under one roof and having sexual relations. Instead of spouses, the individuals agree to be "partners." There is no commitment before God, before the law, or before society. If you are reading this and find yourself in a relationship outside of marriage (no matter what the reason is), our heart is to show you God's grace. God established marriage as a divine covenant, and when we live outside of that covenant, we deny ourselves the abundance He has for us.

Statistics show that the long-term success rate of cohabitation is lower than that of a marriage commitment before a judge or before the church.[1] Even with the low success rate, more young (and not so young) people than ever are choosing to live together outside of marriage. We believe it is for two main reasons:

1. **Lack of knowledge:** Many couples do not understand the value of marriage nor the consequences of living together outside of marriage. It seems like a logical and convenient option. They may say, "We love each other, and that is what counts. A paper is of no value to us." Even those who have grown up in families with traditional values about marriage many times choose to follow what modern culture dictates, including the idea that living together is

---

1. Ahu Gemici and Steve Laufer, "Marriage and Cohabitation" (New York University, September 21, 2011), https://economics.yale.edu/sites/default/files/Workshops-Seminars/Labor-Public/gemici-111006.pdf.

normal. "Everybody does it." They differ from the traditional ideas of their parents and spiritual leaders, and they make decisions on their own, no matter who agrees or disagrees. Most are already sexually involved and feel that they belong to each other. Sometimes they already have children together. Without biblical understanding, there isn't a clear reason to form their family any other way.

2. *Fear:* In many cases couples do not have a good example of what a healthy marriage looks like. They have seen or experienced the pain of their parents' divorce and do not want to have the same result. They think living together without commitment will be a good test run to see if things are going to work out, thus avoiding a failed marriage. Those who live in dysfunctional homes are ready to get away from difficult situations. Women in particular may feel trapped in their family and possibly suffer physical, verbal, or sexual abuse. They want to escape painful situations, and living together seems like a good option to start a new life.

"Seems like" are the key words. In reality, cohabitation is a cheap counterfeit of God's perfect design. One of the consequences of living together is that there is no solid bond beyond feelings, sexual attraction, and promises that have been made to each other. What often keeps these couples together through the years are the children and/or the financial commitments they have made. Women especially desire to feel safe and protected in a stable relationship. However, the last things this option offers are stability and protection. The lack of security can also affect general health and well-being. Research shows that married people live longer and in better health than those who cohabitate without marrying.[2] As time passes, the reasons to stay together lose their relevance, and the daily offenses and lack of trust can cause this type of relationship to fall apart or remain in survival mode.

Another negative consequence is that by not making a commitment before God or society, the spiritual aspect of the relationship is neglected. Without the protective covenant of marriage, the devil has legal access to steal, kill, and destroy what should be a great blessing (John 10:10). Even when a couple starts out with good intentions to love and be faithful, there are spiritual forces working against them, and they are left without weapons to defend themselves. God's desire is to pour His abundance on our lives, but for that to happen we have to align with His will. Living together unmarried is not God's will, and it doesn't carry His blessing.

> For God did not call us to be impure, but to live a holy life. Therefore, anyone who rejects this instruction does not reject a human being but God, the very God who gives you his Holy Spirit (1 Thessalonians 4:7–8).

Contractual Marriage

A contractual marriage is when a couple decides to marry and make their public commitment in a civil ceremony or

---

[2]. Lee A. Lillard and Constantijn (Stan) Panis, "Health, Marriage, and Longer Life for Men," RAND Corporation, January 1, 1998, https://www.rand.org/pubs/research_briefs/RB5018.html. See also "Marriage and Men's Health - Harvard Health Publishing," Harvard Health, June 5, 2019, https://www.health.harvard.edu/mens-health/marriage-and-mens-health.

a religious service. In many countries, the church does not have the jurisdiction to legally marry individuals. In the United States, however, certified spiritual leaders have the legal authority to officiate weddings. Carrying out a civil or religious ceremony is an important step in the formalization of a relationship because it usually reflects a couple's sincere desire to publicly commit to one another. Even our postmodern society still considers it "the right thing to do."

As the definition says, a contractual marriage is based on a contract or legal agreement. Like any contract, it can be terminated with the corresponding penalties. On the legal side, the marriage is recognized before the law and falls under binding legal statutes, which affect personal freedoms, the future of children, and any acquired assets. On the religious side, the tradition is to carry out a celebration depending on spiritual beliefs and family values. I (Luis) was born and raised in Mexico where most people grow up with certain religious traditions. Although church weddings were the norm, I didn't really understand the spiritual significance behind them. I am sure this happens in most cultures.

The religious wedding is often based on the emotions of the dress, guest list, decorations, reception, etc. None of this is wrong, but it overlooks the most important element: the sincere commitment before God, knitting two lives together in Christ. When Christ is not at the center of the union, everything depends on self-effort. God's intention was never to create a marriage contract that depended on the frailty of human agreement. We see the result in the thousands of marriages ended by broken agreements, rescinded promises, separation, and divorce.

"I take you to be my (husband/wife), to have and to hold from this day forward, for better, for worse, for richer, for poorer, in sickness and in health, to love and to cherish, until death do us part. This is my solemn vow." These are more than solemn vows. They are sacred vows, created with the intention of joining two human beings with the divinity of God. But if there is no divine seal, the vows are reduced to eloquent intentions that are difficult, if not impossible, to carry out. And as time passes, those promises are broken, along with the couple's dreams and hearts. We are not saying that a marriage before the law and the church is worthless. Certainly not! It's an important first step toward a successful marriage. But in many cases the recognition of God is absent or added only as a religious adornment, not as the covenant seal of His blessing and presence. These marriages rely solely on human ability to maintain the contract and achieve success.

Covenant Marriage

A divine marriage is a covenant, which is different than a contract. Divine marriage is a covenant before God and with God. It is important to understand what a covenant means. People today use this term as if it were an agreement, like a contract, but according to the Bible it is different. In the Bible, covenants were made before God and sealed with blood, demonstrating the severity of the consequences if they were broken. A story in Genesis 15 illustrates a clear picture of a covenant in the eyes of God. He appears to Abram in a vision, promising him land and abundant offspring. Abram asks God for a confirmation of this promise that seems impossible. He and his wife, Sarah, are childless and beyond childbearing age. God responds by making a covenant with Abram. He asks

Abram to bring animals for a sacrifice and cut them in half. (In Hebrew tradition, covenants were made by blood sacrifice. They would say, "Let us cut a covenant.") The animals were cut in two and the blood drained in the middle. The two people taking the oath walked through the blood. It served as a graphic reminder of what would happen to those who did not fulfill their side of the covenant. In essence they were saying, "My promise is so reliable that I am willing to have the same thing happen to me if I don't keep my word."

Do you think you could trust a promise like that? Well, God's intention for marriage vows was that they would be taken with the same seriousness and awareness of the consequences if broken. Let that sink in a moment. Divorce is deadly, and that's why God says He hates it! (See Malachi 2:16.) You could argue that there are thousands of divorces every day, and there is no blood nor death. But ask a person who is going through a divorce, and you will hear about the heartbreak, the inconsolable crying of their children, the loss of relationships, and the destruction of dreams and desires. It is a death with no funeral, and if you have children together, no closure. It leaves you facing a perilous road ahead that you must navigate day in and day out.

Perhaps you know exactly what we are talking about because you have been there. You have personally experienced that pain. We want to encourage you, because even in the darkness, there is always a ray of hope. So take courage and know that God is the God of restoration (the last chapter of this book is dedicated to blended families and the hope of new beginnings). God knows we cannot keep our promises without His help, and that is why divine marriage covenants are made with Him. In the Genesis 15 story, once Abram divides each animal in half, he expects

God to walk between the sacrifice with him. However, as he waits, he falls into a deep sleep, and what happens next is astonishing: "When the sun had set and darkness had fallen, a smoking firepot and a blazing torch appeared and passed between the pieces. On that day the LORD made a covenant with Abram" (Genesis 15:17-18). Abram did not walk the covenant at all—Jesus took his place! Two torches of fire pass through the sacrifice, coming into agreement and sealing the covenant. We believe those two fires are God the Father and the Son. That means Jesus walked between the sacrifice in Abram's place, vowing to pay the price if the agreement was broken. In the same way, He took our place by paying the price for our sins, shedding His own blood, and facing the death we deserve for not keeping our part of the covenant. Isn't that amazing? How great and merciful is our God!

The key to keeping the divine covenant of marriage is to have Christ at the center of our union. When Jesus is the center, He helps us in our weakness, and we can trust that His blood cleanses our sin. As in the story of Abram, Christ's sacrifice makes it possible for us to keep our part of the covenant, but we have to give Him control of our marriage and do it His way. We must receive the blessing of our heavenly Father through Christ's sacrifice and recognize Jesus as the Savior and Lord of our lives. We do this by declaring with our mouths and believing in our hearts that He was raised from the dead (Romans 10:9-10).

If there is no personal salvation (a divine encounter with God), there will be no divine marriage. The only path that leads to a truly blessed life together is through Jesus the Son of God, who came to free us from the oppression of the devil and paid the ultimate price to save us from our sins. When we accept His lordship and live according to the guidance of the Holy Spirit, not according to our own desires, we are on the road to living a divine marriage with all its blessings and benefits!

Benefits of a Divine Marriage

Revelation of the True Purpose of Marriage

"You're my better half," "You complete me," and other similar sayings sound very romantic, but what we are really saying is that our satisfaction and happiness depend 50 percent on the other person. In reality, though, we are 100 percent responsible for our own happiness, and we receive our true satisfaction from Jesus and being complete in Him. He is the one who takes our brokenness and promises to make us whole. When two whole people unite with Christ, the result is exponential unity. Mathematics in the Kingdom of God is different; 1+1+1 doesn't equal 3. When it comes to marriage, $1+1+1 = 1^3$. Marriage was created by God so we can live a divine reality here on earth, loving and accepting each other as we are, even with our failings. It is God who redeems and sanctifies us.

This is not to say that we should settle for bad attitudes and actions. On the contrary, it means we understand our happiness doesn't depend on our spouse, and we are a part of the redemptive process of God's love in their life. If we let God teach us to love, forgive, and extend grace, then we discover the supernatural moving of the Holy Spirit in our marriage. We connect to a dimension beyond ourselves when we stop living for our own desires and happiness and instead live to be like Christ in our spouse's life. If we humbly seek God together, confessing that we do not know how to build a divine marriage, He will reveal Himself and teach us things we have never seen, thought, or imagined (1 Corinthians 2:9-10). When there is a mutual desire in marriage to seek God and have Him be the center of our lives, everything changes. Our human limitations end, and His divine power begins.

Vision and Direction to Build a Healthy Family

When it comes to starting a family, we all begin with dreams—where we will live, how many children we will have, what kind of house we will buy, and how we will grow old, retire, and travel the world together. Dreaming is great, but if we do not seek God and have a clear plan to achieve those goals, then much of what we hoped for gets lost over time in the daily grind of life. Broken dreams and disappointment are a stark reality. How many couples today, instead of enjoying a peaceful, happy home, experience hell on earth? Sadly, so many couples will not grow old together. Some families have moved so many times that the memories they created are blurred because of financial instability. How many more have only traveled the world online or are still paying for the last trip they made several years ago? Today the only thing they remember about the trip is the monthly payment. Sadly, the answer is far too many. Because there was no clear, God-directed plan, life did not turn out as originally hoped.

There are so many uncertainties in this world. The only hope for security for your family is building your home on the solid rock of Jesus and His Word.

Therefore everyone who hears these words of mine and puts them into practice is like a wise man who built his house on the rock. The rain came down, the streams rose, and the winds blew and beat against that house; yet it did not fall, because it had its foundation on the rock. But everyone who hears these words of mine and does not put them into practice is like a foolish man who built his house on sand (Matthew 7:24-26).

To receive clear vision and direction for your family, begin by seeking God and praying together, writing down what you both want, and then submitting it to the Lord. Pray as Jesus prayed: "Not my will, but yours be done" (Luke 22:42). God has given us important resources to know His will. He has given us His Word that we can study together and apply what it teaches us about relationships, money, children, sex, etc. He has also given us community. Building a healthy home means living outside of ourselves and our own desires. That is why it is so important that we are part of a healthy, holy, and servant-hearted church. We should avoid legalistic, religious churches that place heavy burdens on our family. A great way to build unity at home is serving together as a couple at church and inviting our children to serve and extend the Kingdom of God with us. In this way, we serve others through the family, the church, and the community. Having a divine marriage means having a family vision that focuses on people and activities that have eternal value. The house, trips, schools, clothes, cars, vacations, etc., will arrive in time with God's direction. His Word says that if we seek first the Kingdom of God and His righteousness, everything else will fall into place (see Matthew 6:33). In other words, if we live according to God's will, we have nothing to worry about. He will take care of us. This seems like an easy solution, but it's not. Like everything God does, it is simple, but simple doesn't mean easy. It takes humility to submit our will to God and wait for the Holy Spirit to guide us. And it takes patience and discipline to wait for God to move. We must learn to listen and see with our spiritual senses. That is why we believe marriage is for a lifetime—it takes that long to learn and develop these disciplines!

Together, Kristen and I have lived both ways—our way and God's way. At the beginning of our marriage, it was like a tug of war, each person trying to pull harder in their direction. I must admit that I pulled the hardest. I wanted to do my will and achieve my dreams, goals, and aspirations. I had good intentions, or so I thought. But at the end of the day, I was living my way, according to my will. I thought perhaps God did not care about the insignificant details of our lives, and it depended on me to achieve what I wanted. For many years, even as a Christian, I lived that way. It produced ongoing problems in our relationship and with those around us. Many of my decisions were based on pride, insecurity, ambition, or fear. I thought we were doing our best, and that would be enough. But I was wrong. I discovered that God is highly personal and wants to bless us abundantly. Then, as the saying goes, I "let myself be loved" and began to experience something supernatural. Now, God is in control of our marriage, and we can rest in Him.

We have seen the hand of God move in an amazing way in our family from the smallest details to the most important decisions. We are not perfect by any means, but we are willing to put Him first. We have realized time and again that when we live this way, everything works out for the better. Of course, sometimes we revert to old habits and have moments when pride, fear, and insecurity cast their votes in the decisions of our marriage. When this happens, we quickly return to the feet of Jesus, repent for our actions, receive His love and His forgiveness, and then move on. What a different life! It is truly possible to build a healthy family on the foundation of a divine marriage. It's not crazy; it's a divine dimension, full of His power.

Power to Experience God's Culture: Righteousness, Peace, and Joy

One of the most beautiful things about a divine marriage is reaping the fruit of a relationship with God. If He is the center of our marriage, then we will live His Kingdom here on earth. The Lord's Prayer becomes an everyday reality:

> Your kingdom come, your will be done, on earth [here in our marriage] as it is in heaven (Matthew 6:10).

It is no longer a petition for something we hope for; it's a declaration of a reality in our lives. What does the Kingdom of God look like in marriage? Every kingdom has a culture, with values and customs that characterize it. Romans 14:17 explains that the Kingdom of God and its culture are not about food and drink but about righteousness, peace, and joy in the Holy Spirit. This means that if a marriage has joy, it is because there is peace between them and with God. If there is peace, it is because they are walking in righteousness. For example, if we live according to God's principles and respect each other, there will be no unrighteousness or injustice between us, because respect takes precedence. This will bring peace to our home, which is the environment that cultivates joy and contentment.

On the other hand, when we are unrighteous and act unjustly in selfishness, we lose respect for one another. Peace flies out the window. Instead of joy, there is sadness, despair, discouragement, bitterness, etc. It is easy to tell the difference between a marriage that represents the Kingdom of God and its culture and one that does not. If we want to submit our will to God's principles, we need to do what He says. He tells us that if others offend, then you forgive. If you offend others, then ask for forgiveness.

This world would be so different if we did this more often. But this is hard because of our pride and sinful thoughts. We are not willing to give in when we think we are right. The point is not who is right but who has the humility to talk about the issue without anger and bitterness. Having humility does not mean agreeing on everything but rather being able to take the other person into consideration, listen to their point of view, put the argument before God, and ask for His wisdom to reach the best agreement. (We will see more on this topic in Chapter 6: Conflict Resolution).

Unity in marriage is key. **Without unity there is no profound revelation of God's love in us.** To achieve this unity, we must always maintain the culture of the Kingdom of God above our own ideas and traditions. To maintain this culture of righteousness, peace, and joy, Kristen and I ask ourselves these three questions when making decisions:

1. Is what we want to do fair and honorable?
2. Does it prioritize peace in our family?
3. Will it ultimately bring joy to our home?

If the answer is yes, we go ahead with the plan. When we haven't filtered our decisions by these questions, we have noticed the difference.

Why don't you take a moment to consider what kind of relationship you have? Cohabitation, contractual marriage, or a covenant marriage. Take time to talk about what steps you can take toward a divine marriage, blessed by God and beautiful in its expression. Begin by surrendering your lives to Jesus as Lord and Savior if you have not already done so. Make sure your marriage is under God's leadership. Take the first step, which is simply deciding to do it. Be encouraged and keep in mind what my Mexican abuelita would always tell me: "Mientras haya vida hay esperanza!" ("As long as we are breathing, there is still hope!")

CHAPTER 2
Enemies of Peace

Make every effort to keep yourselves united in the Spirit, binding yourselves together with peace.
—Ephesians 4:3 (NLT)

PEACE IS A VALUABLE GIFT. THE WORLD IS FULL OF afflictions, distractions, and noise. There is nothing more beautiful than coming home and finding peace. Peace gives us the ability to refresh ourselves and regain strength to face the next day. On the other hand, a lack of peace at home deeply affects our health and well-being. Today we see an epidemic in cases of depression, anxiety, panic, and suicide. It's undeniable that a spirit of fear has been unleashed in our society. The way we combat that fear is through peace. Jesus said, "I am leaving you with a gift—peace of mind and heart. And the peace I give is a gift the world cannot give. So don't be troubled or afraid" (John 14:27 NLT).

How many times have we said, "I just need some peace and quiet"? We were made in the image and likeness of God, and God is peace. It is not in our God-given nature to live in discord or conflict. It may seem counterintuitive, but you have to fight for peace. There is spiritual warfare against peace in our marriages and families, and there is a reason for that. Remember that a divine marriage should be the representation of the Kingdom of God here on earth, and the Bible describes the Kingdom of God as righteousness, peace, and joy (Romans 14:17). One of the reasons the devil will try to steal our peace is to prevent us from representing God correctly. The devil knows that if he can steal our peace, he can also steal our joy. Joy is the result of a life of righteousness and peace. It is different than happiness. The motivation of many couples is to get married and live "happily ever after." There is nothing wrong with that; God wants us to be happy together. But joy in the Kingdom of God is different from the happiness this world offers. The happiness of this world is external, and we receive it from what we can see, hear, smell, taste, or touch—our five senses. Such happiness only lasts for a finite period of time. However, the joy of the Lord, which is our strength, comes from within our being—from the fullness of the soul, from knowing who we are and to whom we belong. It comes from our inner peace, and unlike worldly happiness, it is eternal. Jesus says He is our peace. He is the Prince of Peace (Isaiah 9:6). Jesus does not give us peace like the world does (John 14:27); His peace surpasses all understanding (Philippians 4:7). In other words, the peace of God is not of this world. It is supernatural! (See John 16:33.)

As a couple, we must vigilantly guard the peace in our marriage. We have to resist the attacks that come against us. Anything that robs our peace is not worth pursuing or tolerating. There are several factors that affect peace, and if we identify them as enemies of our home, we will have the motivation to be vigilant in protecting our marriage. Let us look at several sinister enemies of peace that we need to identify and resist:

- selfishness
- lack of rest
- anger and addictions
- mismanagement of money
- unresolved relational conflicts
- chronic illness
- misuse of social media
- fear of the unknown

Selfishness

When we are selfish, we create an atmosphere of tension. Everything revolves around us, and we are not aware of the physical, emotional, and spiritual needs of our spouse. This leaves our spouse vulnerable to insecurity that robs their peace, and we both suffer. When we are self-centered, we don't really care how the other person feels or if our actions are affecting our relationship. We say that we do, but our actions contradict our words. We are insensitive to how our selfishness affects the atmosphere in our home, and we exchange living in peace for what pleases us in the moment. The spiritual entity behind selfishness is pride. When we give it spiritual authority in our lives, the end result is devastating.

Jesus invites us in Matthew 11:29 to be like Him, "gentle and humble in heart." When we are gentle and humble, we think of our spouse first. Giving them priority fosters peace because we are aware of their feelings and needs. I invite you to begin practically and proactively thinking of your spouse first today. Before deciding to do something your way, think about how it would affect peace in your marriage.

Lack of Rest

This is one of the most common yet overlooked factors that affects our peace. It is like that elephant in the room that everyone knows exists but no one talks about. When we do not get enough rest from our activities or enough sleep, we set ourselves up for conflict. When we are tired, we are less tolerant and more impatient. We get irritated easily and overreact to situations that are not worth getting upset about.

Excess work is a deceptive thief that masquerades as responsibility. A responsible provider desires to stabilize their family's lives financially and provide for their needs and desires. That is a good thing, unless you are exchanging it for peace. Kristen and I have learned that more is not always better. When we value our peace, we value rest. God values rest as well, and He commands us to take at least one day a week to rest from our jobs and daily routines:

> Remember the Sabbath day by keeping it holy. Six days you shall labor and do all your work, but the seventh day is a sabbath to the LORD your God. On it you shall not do any work (Exodus 20:8).

God Himself rested on the seventh day after finishing Creation. Why would He have to rest if He is all powerful? God rested not because He was tired but because He was done.

Enemies of Peace

Our work should have cycles that begin and end. We start a week and end on a certain day. We rest for a day or two and then start over. Yes, it's true that "work is never done"— it will always be there waiting. However, not taking a break will negatively affect our health and relationships. Many complaints come from women who feel their husbands are never home. A husband may answer this complaint with, "But I do it for you and the kids! You have everything you need, don't you?" The answer is no, she doesn't. She is lacking peace. The peace of having her husband at home, taking a walk in the park, eating together, sharing popcorn and their favorite show, watching Dad play with the kids... just being there. Remember, we got married to be together, but if we work all day every day, then we undermine the reason we got married in the first place.

I (Luis) remember that when my children were young, I worked long hours, trying to get a new business off the ground. I left early while they were still asleep and came home when they were already in bed. I would arrive late for their birthdays and recitals or not make it at all. Kristen felt like a single parent, and it was hard on her. I even remember coming home late on Christmas one year to find our family and guests patiently waiting for me at the table as dinner was already served. Enough was enough. I had missed so many magical moments that I could never get back. Was it worth it? Of course not! I invested the best of myself in a business I no longer even have. Thankfully, I came to my senses before it was too late. I worked on prioritizing my schedule and brought peace and joy back to our home.

Pause for a moment and analyze your life. How fast are you going? Is it worth the extra income if it sabotages your peace? Overworking adds unneeded stress to the relationship and leads to conflicts, anger, and frustration. Think about this:

when someone is on their deathbed, they never say, "Why didn't I make more money? Why didn't I spend more time at work?" No, they think, *Why didn't I spend more time with my family? Why didn't I make time to walk in the park with my wife? I should have played more with my children and listened to them.* Friends, let's be aware of this and make more time to rest and enjoy family life. If not, we will live with regret.

Anger and Addictions

Anger is one of the fiercest enemies contending against our peace. If there are arguments, shouting, or outbursts of anger, then peace leaves the room! The Bible wisely tells us,

> Better a dry crust with peace and quiet
> than a house full of feasting, with strife
> (Proverbs 17:1).

We're all guilty of feeling angry at some point in our married lives. I am certainly guilty of allowing my emotions to get the better of me and getting angry over things that are not very important. God tells us that we can be angry without sinning (see Ephesians 4:26). How is that possible? God is speaking here about anger against the injustice that affects our lives and that of others—not anger when we lose control and lash out. We can get angry at sin and disagree with someone but not vent our anger. This is only possible, though, with the help of the Holy Spirit, since to control anger, we need to have self-control. Self-control is a fruit of the Holy Spirit; it is not an act of the will (Galatians 5:22–23).

We must not allow anger, which is a spirit, to control our emotions. As Kristen wrote in the introduction to this book, evil lurks like a roaring lion looking for someone to devour (see 1 Peter 5:8). Anger is like that lion that devours our peace in marriage and in our relationship with our children. Anger is a symptom, not a disease. It is an alarm, alerting us to deeper issues. We can be freed from anger by addressing the root. Ask the Lord for revelation in this area. Possible root causes include insecurity, fear, disappointment, and bitterness. God warns us not to let bitterness take root within us:

> Get rid of all bitterness, rage, anger, harsh words, and slander, as well as all types of evil behavior. Instead, be kind to each other, tenderhearted, forgiving one another, just as God through Christ has forgiven you (Ephesians 4:31–32 NLT).

Anger and addictions go hand in hand. One usually opens the door for the other. Addictions are deceptive, often beginning as something that seems insignificant. Over time, though, they take control of our emotions and our will. God exhorts us through His Word not to allow ourselves to be dominated by anything but to submit all thoughts and actions to Him. In general, addictions are an attempt to escape undesirable situations such as work pressures, relationship conflicts, emotional issues, stress, boredom, discouragement, etc. Once addictions take root in our mind and body, it is difficult (but thankfully not impossible) to break them. They can include dependencies on things like television, social media, food, pornography, alcohol, and legal or illegal drugs. I remember a time many years ago when a friend had a secret addiction to cocaine. None of us knew, because he seemed to have everything going for him—a successful career, an outgoing personality, good looks, and a beautiful wife. They were newlyweds, and she knew nothing about his dark secret. He was able to hide his addiction from co-workers, friends, and family. As time went by, my friend realized he no longer had enough money to support his habit, so he began stealing. He started subtly taking things from their home and selling them. When he couldn't cover his tracks anymore at home, he began stealing from his in-laws' home. By the time he confessed, the damage was irreparable. His wife's family decided not to press charges, but my friend lost both his professional license and his marriage.

Sadly, this tragic story is not uncommon. Addictions are a tool of the devourer. The enemy uses them to steal your peace, health, marriage, career, relationships, and in many cases, even your life. A person with addictions needs immediate help. If you are struggling with anything that has a hold on you, you cannot play with fire and not get burned. The key to freedom is to recognize that you are not in control. Bring the addiction out of the darkness. Talk to your spouse and get help. Whenever someone is willing to change and receive help, there is always hope. Do something about it today!

Mismanagement of Money

There is a well-known saying in Mexico: "Cuando el dinero sale por la puerta, el amor se va por la ventana." ("When money runs out the door, love goes out the window.") Another is, "¡Hasta que las deudas nos separen!" ("Until debt do us part!") These sayings may sound amusing, but there is a sad truth to both. Overwhelming debt, bad financial planning, and the absence of a budget all cause high stress on a marriage and rob our peace. The apostle Paul wrote, "For the love of money is the root of all kinds of evil. And some people, craving money, have wandered from the true faith and pierced themselves with many sorrows" (1 Timothy 6:10 NLT). Kristen and I lived through those "many sorrows" because of poor financial planning. We came into our marriage with very different views on money. We naively thought it was not a big deal to think differently about it. As time went by, though, we realized it was causing a tremendous amount of conflict. For example, Kristen thought money was to be saved, and I thought money was to be spent. All of this came from the different backgrounds in which we grew up. Kristen grew up in a financially difficult situation. Her dad left home when she was young, and her mom had to work hard to raise her and her siblings alone. Her background was working hard to get by and saving what little was left.

I also came from a dysfunctional family, but my situation was different. I left home when I was 13 years old, and I had to fend for myself. I longed to have all the things I thought I was missing. I lived day to day not knowing where I would sleep each night. For those reasons my concept of money was, "If you have it, spend it, because who knows what will happen tomorrow!" One thing I have learned the hard way is that it doesn't matter how much you earn. What really matters is how much you spend. No matter how much money we have, if we spend more than we earn, we are in trouble. Sooner or later the difference will catch up with us. Poor financial management creates insecurity and mistrust in our relationship. Not knowing where we stand financially along with the horrible pressures of debt can lead to serious conflict in a marriage. God has taught us a lot about this topic, and in Chapter 7: Money Matters, we will talk more about it. For the moment, I can tell you that God always wants to be included in our finances. Receiving His guidance can make all the difference in transforming a stressed and anxious marriage into a happy and peaceful one.

Unresolved Relational Conflicts

Let's talk about broken relationships. We were created to have deep relationships with our parents, children, siblings, relatives, friends, co-workers, etc. God made us relational because He is relational. But when relationships break down (for whatever reason), they leave deep emotional wounds and affect us as a couple. When relationships with other family members are strained, they cause conflicts in the marriage and affect the whole family. These situations can begin with a seemingly insignificant offense that, when left unresolved, can grow to the point of family members refusing to speak to one another. It is especially damaging when the conflict is with the in-laws. This causes tension for the spouse who was not involved in the conflict and makes them feel caught in the middle. There is an expectation to defend their spouse no matter who was in the wrong. It is difficult to maneuver, and no matter what is said or done, it usually is perceived as the wrong thing or not enough. There are couples who have had problems with family members for years. In the end, no one wins—everyone loses. This can also happen with friends and church family. It is sad to see and even worse to experience this type of conflict. The consequences of not forgiving are costly. It is always worth the effort to make steps toward reconciliation:

> Love prospers when a fault is forgiven,
> but dwelling on it separates close friends
> (Proverbs 17:9 NLT).

One thing I have learned in our marriage is that conflict in any relationship is going to affect Kristen emotionally in a profound way. In general, women are more concerned about the health of their relationships than men. Most men can move on quickly without resolving broken relationships, but women are affected deeply by having conflict with the people they love. Women tend to feel greater satisfaction in life when their relationships are healthy, whereas men feel satisfied through personal achievement. It is not that women are emotionally weaker than men. On the contrary, women have incredible inner fortitude, yet they are more sensitive. Men, on the other hand, tend to be insensitive and proud. I can assure you, based on my own experience, that when you take the initiative to restore relationships with your family and friends, your spouse will thank you.

If you want to have a peaceful marriage, take steps toward restoring broken relationships, no matter who is at fault. Someone needs to take the first step, so why not let it be you? Don't let the devil steal the blessing of your relationships. I've heard it said, "A man is rich not because of his money, but because of his friendships." Let's live in peace with everyone!

Chronic Illness

When someone struggles with a chronic illness, it affects so many areas of the marriage relationship, such as day-to-day activities, finances, and intimacy. It can also create an emotional toll of despair, frustration, anger, sadness, hopelessness, selfishness, rejection, etc.

Sickness is something that can affect us all. It is important to know it's not God's desire for us to be sick (see Psalm 103:1–5). However, we live in a fallen world, and part of the result of original sin is sickness. Thankfully, God has given us resources, both natural and spiritual, to deal with illness. He tells us that by His stripes we have been healed, and we are now free from all oppression and affliction (Isaiah 53:5). In the process of understanding and living this truth, we must keep our peace. Jesus said," I have told you all this so that you may have peace in me. Here on earth you will have many trials and sorrows. But take heart, because I have overcome the world" (John 16:33 NLT). When we do not have the peace that only He can give, a peace that passes all understanding, we suffer greater affliction. But when we receive God's supernatural peace and love, we can in turn give His peace and love to help heal our loved one's pain. It is challenging to walk through life together when you or your spouse are suffering from an illness. There is nothing more important in difficult times in our marriage than knowing we can count on each other.

> Two people are better off than one, for they can help each other succeed. If one person falls, the other can reach out and help. But someone who falls alone is in real trouble. Likewise, two people lying close together can keep each other warm. But how can one be warm alone? A person standing alone can be attacked and defeated, but two can stand back-to-back and conquer. Three are even better, for a triple-braided cord is not easily broken (Ecclesiastes 4:9-12 NLT).

This portion of Scripture is well known, and we have heard it at many weddings, but perhaps we do not fully understand its power. The key to receiving the strength we need is found in the last verse. If we invite God to be the center of our marriage, then His Holy Spirit is the third strand in the cord. And if God is with us, who can be against us? Kristen and I have personally lived through difficult health situations, and we can testify that His power is real. With

God, everything is possible. If you are going through a time of physical affliction, then I encourage you and your spouse to pray for His strength, peace, and the revelation of His truth, which is the Word of God. (I also highly recommend Kristen's book *Keys of the Kingdom*, which is a prayer guide specifically geared toward experiencing breakthroughs in the areas of emotional and physical health).[3]

Misuse of Social Media

Technology can be a blessing or a curse—it all depends on how we handle it. Like money, it should be a tool to make our life easier, not something that controls us. What starts out as a recreational activity can unexpectedly turn into a serious problem or even an addiction because of the lack of self-control. The most dangerous thing about this kind of addiction is that it doesn't feel like one. It is not like alcohol or drugs that have noticeable symptoms. Excessive use of the internet and social media is more subtle. You can disguise it as work or simply as a distraction and entertainment. For many people, social media fills an acceptance void. (Although, ironically, I think the more "likes" you have on social media, the lonelier you feel since most of those "friends" are simply illusions of belonging to someone.) No matter the motivations, we all know social media is highly addictive if we don't set limits. If you want your spouse and children not to stare at a screen all the time, then it starts with you. For example, if you are eating, don't have your mobile phone or tablet on the table. Set specific times to use social media. Keep communication open. Don't have

---

3. Kristen Román, *Keys of the Kingdom: 21 Day Prayer Guide to Breakthrough* (Dallas, TX: Exito en la Familia, 2019).

passwords on your phone, and if you do, it is important that your spouse and children know them. That way you keep yourself accountable for your social media activity.

It is important to remember that what you do not only affects you but also your marriage and family. In time it will bear visible fruit. When we get married, we become one, interconnected in body, soul, and spirit. This means that what I watch, read, and listen to affects my spouse in some way, whether positively or negatively. One of the most important benefits of marriage is intimacy, because it is an exclusive place for three persons. *Three?* you may wonder. A place for three persons sounds strange, but we are talking about a divine marriage in which God is the center. For this reason there are three persons: you, your spouse, and the Holy Spirit. When we are not careful about what we watch, read, and listen to, we allow other things or people to invade our intimate place. Years ago, we were warned to be careful with television, as it could negatively influence our home and marriage. Today, the negative influence through social media is much more aggressive. The world is in our hands, and the temptation is great, not only for young people but also for adults. It is incredible to have so much information at our fingertips. Sure, technology is a great blessing, but without self-control it is a destructive force. The stories of infidelity because of connections and reconnections on social media platforms are too numerous to count.

One practical suggestion is to have your social media accounts together as a couple so that both of you have access to everything you are seeing and saying. Our enemy is very cunning, and he attacks when we least expect it. Here is an example: after a conflict with your spouse that left you feeling angry and emotionally separated, you grab your phone and open social media to forget the situation. Suddenly, you receive a message: "Hi! How are you?" It's your old flame from high school. It seems harmless, so you start to engage in a conversation without any wrong intentions. But at that moment you are emotionally vulnerable. The conversation can continue for moments and then hours, days, months, etc., until the opportunity arises to reconnect in person with someone who made you feel good in the past and is now a welcome distraction from the routine of conflicts that exist in your marriage. And the rest is history.

Very few people intentionally plan an affair, so how does it happen? Opening the door to social media seems harmless. But imagine if that same person knocks on the front door of your house and you eagerly invite them in, knowing that your spouse is at home. After talking and reconnecting for a while, you feel a mutual attraction and invite them to come visit as many times as they want—in the morning, afternoon, or late at night ... even if your spouse is not at home. Obviously, this is a formula for disaster!

We must guard our marriage from these temptations. Just as it can be an old friend or even a stranger whom you invite into the privacy of your home through social media, it can also be pornography, video games, funny videos, or excessive information that has you glued to your screen. Or maybe you love to know the how and why of things, so Google becomes your constant companion. Many of us spend more time with our phone or tablet than an actual person. If this is your case, we suggest making a hard stop. Try a media fast to allow your mind to detox. Pause your Facebook, Instagram, Twitter, etc., for a while. Close the door and invite your spouse to help you keep it shut. You will be surprised with how much time you will have to connect with each other. Remember, we are not against social media; it is a tool that can be used for good as long as it doesn't control us.

Fear of the Unknown

Fear constantly stalks us. If we lower our guard and allow it to speak to our thoughts, then we fall into the uncertainty of "What if this or that happens?" Our mind begins a downward spiral into catastrophic thinking. Living in fear can paralyze the hopes and dreams we have for our marriage. The devil wants to immobilize us with fear.

Fear is worrying about something that has not happened and may not ever happen. When we face fear alone, we will surely be overcome, but when we face it with the Spirit of God, we will surely overcome. Second Timothy 2:7 says, "For God has not given us a spirit of fear and timidity, but of power, love, and self-discipline" (NLT). The key to overcoming fear is having the discipline to keep our minds focused on the love of God: "There is no fear in love. But perfect love drives out fear" (1 John 4:17–18).

When we experience fear, the important thing is not to have more courage but to have more love! God has promised not to leave us or abandon us in any situation (see Romans 8:31–39). It is important to share our fears with our spouse and pray together. It is not easy when we feel vulnerable, but it is critical. The disciplines of reading the Word and prayer are key to overcoming any fear. Remember that the Bible says two are better than one, and a triple braided cord is not easily broken (see Ecclesiastes 4:12). It is possible to defeat the enemies against us if we are intentionally united with the Lord and each other, making every effort to live in peace.

CHAPTER 3
Our **Differences** Are Our **Strengths**

Two people are better off than one,
for they can help each other succeed.
—Ecclesiastes 4:9 (NLT)

WHEN LUIS AND I MET EACH OTHER, WE THOUGHT we were exactly alike. Now it makes me laugh because the truth is, we are very different. Obviously, we have things in common, and we think alike about the most important values in life. That is what attracted us to one another. But the ways we navigate everyday life are completely different. Dealing with these differences in our daily life together has been a great challenge. Not only with the simple, less important things, like arguing over the thermostat or who took the longest in the bathroom, but also with more important things, like money, sex, and order in the house. Honestly, there was a time when I thought our differences were going to separate us forever. But thank God, at our worst moments, when the temptation to pack up and leave was a real struggle, I had a moment of clarity, an epiphany. I remember my desperate cry to God: "Why did You make us so different? Why can't Luis see things like I do?" (As if I were the model of perfection, and it was God's fault for not creating him in my flawless image!) God answered by opening my eyes. I saw something that because of my selfishness and pain I had not seen before: our differences are our strengths. Being so different is a positive thing. In fact, it is a blessing! Before, I saw it as something negative, that in a good moment I tolerated and in a bad moment I resented. However, being different provides an opportunity to grow. And as we know from the laws of nature, the moment we stop growing, we start dying. Everything healthy grows. I realized the key was in my attitude and the perspective I chose. Our attitude is our responsibility. We cannot blame God, the enemy, or our spouse.

Statistics tell us the main reasons behind the majority of divorces are not extreme situations like addictions, abuse, infidelity, etc. Instead, they are the lack of commitment and the inability to resolve differences.[4] The way we navigate our differences is key to the success of our marriage. When we marry, we need to face three types of important differences:

1. Gender
2. Family culture
3. Personality

---

4. Alan J. Hawkins and Tamara A. Fackrell, *Should I Keep Trying to Work It Out?: A Guidebook for Individuals and Couples at the Crossroads of Divorce (and before)* (Salt Lake City, UT: Produced on behalf of the Utah Commission on Marriage, 2009).

There have been many studies and surveys made to identify the differences between the basic needs of men and women, and the results speak louder than any argument for gender neutrality. No one can successfully argue that men and women are essentially the same. We are not! We have the same intrinsic value as human beings, but God created us male and female for a reason. There are multiple ways to group the results of these surveys, but I like how Jimmy Evans lists them in his book *Marriage on the Rock*. The needs are listed in order of importance.

For men:
1. Honor
2. Sex
3. Friendship with their wives
4. Domestic support

For women:
1. Security
2. Soft, nonsexual affection
3. Open and honest communication
4. Leadership[5]

This doesn't mean that a woman doesn't need honor and sexual fulfillment, or that a man doesn't desire security and nonsexual affection. It simply puts them in the order of priority. It helps us evaluate if we are loving our spouse in a way that makes them feel loved and fulfilled. We often think we are being loving and attentive, but we are doing it in a way that makes *us* (not our spouse) feel good. We can waste

---

5. Jimmy Evans, *Marriage on the Rock* (Dallas, TX: XO Publishing, 1994), 125–137, 170–183.

emotional energy and not see the results we hope for (such as gratitude and satisfaction) because our spouse doesn't perceive our loving attempts in the same way.

Another important difference is family culture. Every family has its own culture: the way we speak (reserved or high strung), the way we show affection (very little or big on hugs), the way we celebrate (with few or many traditions), the way we eat (simple or sophisticated)... the list goes on. Our family culture affects us more than we can imagine. We get used to a certain way of doing things (normally the way our father or mother taught us), and when we arrive at the altar, we bring these customs with us. This reminds me of a funny story that happened when Luis and I were newlyweds. I decided to surprise him with a traditional Mexican dish, and I asked his mother for the recipe for chilaquiles rojos (one of his favorites). When Luis came home for dinner, I was quite pleased with myself and proudly announced that we were having chilaquiles. (I later learned that it is a traditional breakfast dish, but anyway...) Luis walked over to the perfectly clean stove and asked where they were. Chilaquiles are made by frying tortilla strips on the stove and then adding the salsa, cream, etc. "Here they are!" I exclaimed with an excited grin as I pulled a casserole dish out of the oven. I'll never forget his confused expression that turned to obvious disappointment when he tried my new creation: chilaquiles souffle! Growing up, my family didn't fry food or use cooking oil very often because healthy eating was a priority. So when my mother-in-law gave me the recipe, I thought I could improve it by removing the fat and baking the dish instead. As you can imagine, Luis was less than thrilled by my desecrating a sacred culinary tradition!

We have so many stories of differences in our family cultures that we laugh about them now. But small differences can become serious points of conflict. We know a couple who divorced, and the main reason was their differences in punctuality. He could not tolerate the fact that they were always late because she didn't leave enough time to get ready. She grew up in a relaxed family environment in which punctuality wasn't a priority. Tardiness was a habit, and it was stressful for her to feel rushed. He, on the other hand, grew up in a military family in which arriving even a few minutes late was unacceptable and shameful. It is sad to think a relationship could end because of a seemingly small difference, but these types of situations are more common than you would imagine.

The third type of difference is our unique personalities. This is the magnet in "opposites attract." But time passes, and what was once cute, interesting, and attractive is now annoying, offensive, and embarrassing. Usually, the other person hasn't changed at all. What changed are our perspective and attitude. That quiet guy is still quiet, but now his wife complains that he doesn't open up enough. When they were dating, she admired the way he patiently listened to her without interrupting. Now she is bothered that he doesn't talk. But she chose him that way. Then there is the guy who was enthralled by his girlfriend's sense of adventure and independent spirit. But now that she is his wife, he resents the fact that she would rather be out and about than at home. Again, he chose her that way. In our case, I thought it was cute the way Luis had his closet organized by color and that he had a pair of shoes to match every outfit. I, on the other hand, would buy a blouse from the thrift store and then not be able to find it because it was in my pajama drawer! It was cute until Luis wanted me to keep my side of the closet the same way as his! When we were dating, we thought these differences in personality were interesting and fun, but later they almost ended our marriage. To be where we are today, 29 years in and happily still together, we had to work on changing our attitudes and perspectives. It's so important to remember these three things:

1. Being different helps us grow.
2. Being different helps us reflect the image of God.
3. Being different helps us heal.

Being Different Helps Us Grow

I (Kristen) admit I have a hard time with organization. I prefer fun and relaxed environments. When our kids were young, I let them play freely without picking up their toys until the end of the day when they had finished creating their fantasy worlds. The disorder did not bother me, because I considered it a sign of creativity and life. Luis would come home, expecting everything to be in complete order with nothing out of place and would get quite upset if it wasn't. (My husband has changed a lot since those days. He still desires things to be orderly, but his attitude has improved, and so has mine!) There were days when the boys and I managed to pick up everything on time, but there were other days when we didn't. The fighting that ensued was damaging for the whole family. I felt like Luis demanded an impossible level of perfection, and nothing I did was good enough. He felt frustrated and unloved when I didn't take the time to think about what he wanted. We now understand the emotional dynamics, but it took years to be able to articulate those sentiments constructively: "I feel like I am unable to please you when..." and "I don't feel respected when..." Back then, we just felt hurt and angry. I got to the point of feeling fearful and anxious when it was time for Luis to come home. And over time my heart grew bitter. Things started to change, though, when I understood that this area of our marriage that felt like a curse was actually a blessing. I needed more order in my life. That part of Luis's personality was essentially good, but because of his painful childhood experiences, it was out of control. The enemy gained access through the pain and took control of that area of his emotions. Luis later went through spiritual deliverance and was able to find freedom and walk in self-control.

I worked on changing my attitude and perspective so I could also be free. It helped me to reflect on the fact that each personality has an inherent set of strengths and weaknesses. There is no perfect human being. (And all married people say, "Amen!" to that.) Seriously, there is no one with only positive qualities. I remember years ago when Luis and I took a personality test. In that model there were four personality types, and each type had its corresponding set of positive and negative qualities. For example, people with my personality are happy, funny, creative, and relaxed, and we enjoy being with people. Sounds perfect, right? But on the other side of the coin, we tend to be disorganized, indecisive, anxious, and unmotivated. It doesn't sound so perfect anymore!

Understanding that each personality has inherent weaknesses is not an excuse to say, "You see? That's just the way I am, so I can't change." Of course we can change! That's what life in God is all about. In Him we are a new creation. When we are born again, we start a process of sanctification day by day to be more like Him. In my case, I recognized that God wanted to use Luis to help me overcome my weaknesses, because he does not struggle in those areas. I had to humble myself and acknowledge that I needed to be more orderly. As I mentioned before, the way Luis expressed himself in frustration and anger was not from God. But his ability to order things was. And it happens vice versa as well. God wants to use my strengths to help my husband overcome his areas of weakness. I had to face the hard truth that I had chosen my husband as he was. I admire his leadership, his initiative, his entrepreneurial spirit, his courage, and so many other character traits. But those amazing features also come with inherent weaknesses. If I want to enjoy his strengths, then I have to be willing to live with his weaknesses as well. If we do not accept that truth, then we are deceiving ourselves. I don't want to sound like a pessimist, but there is no such thing as a perfect soul mate. And even if they did exist, it wouldn't do you any good to be with them. What's the use of being with someone just like you? The idea is to be a complement, or rather a supplement, to magnify the image of God on earth, not limit it to your image.

Being Different Helps Us Reflect the Glory of God

God is loving, powerful, strong, just, compassionate… the list goes on and on. The Bible says we are made in His image. Every human being reflects some part of the nature of God, and together we magnify that image! If we were the same, it would reduce the impact of the image of God the world sees. Of course, not everything we are reflects the image of God. He deposits in each person His gifts and qualities, but the enemy works to corrupt that image. The last thing the devil wants is for the world to see God's love clearly reflected in marriage. When we are selfish, our positive qualities (like Luis' sense of order and my creativity) can become negative. We make them an idol by giving more importance to that attribute or need in us than to God or the people we love. We say things like:

- "I need ..."
- "I cannot live without ..."
- "I feel empty when I can't ..."
- "You don't understand who I am."
- "I feel like we no longer have anything in common."

Emotions are real, but that doesn't mean they are right. Two very different people can live happily together when they appreciate and value their differences rather than demanding things be done their way. Pride and selfishness are the real enemies of happiness in marriage, not our differences.

One of the legal justifications given for divorce is "irreconcilable differences," but it should be called "irreconcilable selfishness." When you are willing to change your perspective and love as God loves, differences are no longer a problem. Instead, they are a blessing. When we are not clinging to our way of doing things, we can participate in God's *agape* love. Every Christian marriage has the mission of representing the Kingdom of God on earth. We must understand that there is a spiritual battle around this representation. Satan has not changed his strategy. From the beginning in the Garden of Eden, his goal was to distort the image of God. The enemy's message to Eve was, "You see, God is not that good. There is something you need that He does not want to give you." And every time there is a divorce, the enemy shouts to the world, "You see, God is not good. His love is not enough. His plan doesn't work. There is something else you need to be happy, but He doesn't want to give it to you. You'll have to find it somewhere else or with someone else." In Ephesians 5 we read,

> "For this reason a man will leave his father and mother and be united to his wife, and the two will become one flesh." This is a profound mystery—but I am talking about Christ and the church (vv. 31–32).

God's plan is for marriage to be the representation of the love between Christ and His church. The enemy's plan is to sabotage that representation so that the world says, "They are followers of Jesus, but look at how they hurt each other. Certainly, God is not so good." Many children who grow up in Christian homes with conflict and strife later reject their faith because they heard about the love of God but did not see that love lived out in their parents' relationship.

The Bible says the love of God is *agape* love, which is a Greek word that implies fidelity, commitment, and an act of the will. In order to embrace and celebrate our spouse's differences, we need *agape* love. It is the kind of love we do not have naturally. It is the supernatural love in 1 Corinthians 13:4–7:

> Love is patient, love is kind. It does not envy, it does not boast, it is not proud. It does not dishonor others, it is not self-seeking, it is not easily angered, it keeps no record of wrongs. Love does not delight in evil but rejoices with the truth. It always protects, always trusts, always hopes, always perseveres.

Being different gives us the opportunity to humble ourselves and express unconditional, divine love. When we celebrate our differences, we are celebrating the image of our great God revealed in our partner's life. But when we criticize, mock, manipulate, and control our spouse, we distort that image, acting as a pawn in the enemy's hands. It is so important to free our spouse to become who God created them to be so that His glory shines in their life—not only for their own benefit but also to reflect the image of our beautiful God to a world so in need of His love.

Being Different Helps Us Heal

I want to emphasize that throughout this chapter I am talking about differences in personality and temperament and the importance of feeling accepted and affirmed for who we are. I'm not talking about affirming everything we do, especially sinful behavior. The goal is to love one another as Christ loved us. Jesus loves us just as we are, but obviously He does not love everything we do, nor does He affirm everything we do. Appreciating our differences is not saying, "I love the fact that my husband drinks too much and curses up a storm" or "I so appreciate it when my wife criticizes people and gossips." No, those are areas of sin and weakness in which everyone is responsible before God to find freedom. So often, the doors to demonic activity in our lives are opened due to painful experiences. Pain is one of the avenues the enemy uses to access our heart.

When we go through something emotionally painful, there is a great temptation to isolate ourselves and let our emotions run wild, like an injured animal that hides and starts licking its wounds. This is how we look in the spirit when we are hurt: hiding in a corner, licking our wounds, replaying again and again in our minds the painful situation we just experienced. At that moment we are easy prey for the enemy. That is why it is important to stay connected with people who love us even when the temptation is to do the opposite. Another example from nature is how lions stalk their prey. They watch the gazelle herd carefully, patiently, waiting for one to fall behind. They do not have the power to attack the entire herd, so they stalk and wait for a moment of weakness. God's idea for marriage and family is to be a protective herd, even if you feel like Sid in the movie *Ice Age*: "I don't know about you guys, but we are the weirdest herd I have ever seen!"[6] The same is true for our church family (but that's a whole other book!). The idea is to have a place of protection, a refuge, where you can go to heal when you are hurt.

Sadly, in many cases, home is where we experience the most pain. Marriage can feel like a war zone instead of a safe place to recover from the battle outside. Remember what it says in Ecclesiastes:

> A person standing alone can be attacked and defeated, but two can stand back-to-back and conquer. Three are even better, for a triple-braided cord is not easily broken (4:12 NLT).

The key to being people God uses to heal each other and to defeat the enemy together is in the phrase, "Three are even better." If your marriage is not a place of healing, then you need to invite the Holy Spirit to teach you how to change it. There are deep wounds that only God can heal, but He still invites us into the process of having our loving touch and comforting words minister to those hurting areas

---

6. *Ice Age* (Twentieth Century Fox Film Corporation, 2002).

of our spouse's heart. Being different gives us the ability to be strong when our spouse is weak.

Another great Mexican saying is, "Gracias a Dios que no cojeamos de la misma pata." ("Thank God we don't limp with the same leg.") We can bring clarity and a new perspective to each other's pain. "If one person falls, the other can reach out and help" (Ecclesiastes 4:10 NLT). When Luis and I were newly married, I was struggling with relationships in my family. We both come from families broken by our parents' divorces. I was struggling to navigate the complicated relationship I had with my dad and his new wife. I still suffered the pain of his rejection and abandonment. Thankfully, Luis saw things more clearly than I did and was able to give me good advice on how to heal that broken relationship. I also realized through that situation that the same rejection I felt from my dad before meeting Luis influenced my attraction to guys who were not affectionate, expressive, or attentive. When I met Luis, it was difficult for me to receive his affection. He was different from anyone else I had dated. But that difference is what God used to heal my heart from the wound of abandonment. My relationship with my dad is restored today, praise God! I have been able to forgive and find freedom, which allows me to stretch out my arms and offer grace to my father who was carrying his own wounds.

The idea of healing each other sounds great, and maybe we understand it in our mind theoretically, but at some point, it must drop into our heart. God gave us emotions to bless our lives and to help us experience life fully. Many times, though, our emotions betray us, making us feel depressed when nothing is wrong, rejected for no apparent reason, and frustrated with our spouse when in reality we know what happened is not a big deal. When our emotions scream louder than our reason, we need to ask the Holy Spirit if there is a spiritual force working against us. As Christians we should have self-control, which is a fruit of the Holy Spirit. If you don't have it, find out where you left it! Luis has a saying that is so true: "If you lose control, someone else is going to take it." And believe me, that someone does not have your good in mind. He is a thief who comes to steal, kill, and destroy (John 10:10).

Do you remember the beginning of this chapter when I mentioned that Luis had to be delivered in order to change? The word deliverance can scare us and remind us of disturbing images from horror movies, yet true biblical deliverance is simple and should be common in the life of a Christian. I think of it like washing our feet as Jesus mentioned in John 13:10. Getting our feet dirty while we walk through this world is inevitable. But it is so important that we wash ourselves with the Word of God to cleanse ourselves of any unclean spirit that wants to gain access to our life. Just as the disciples were commanded by the Lord to wash each other's feet, there are times when we need help to experience freedom. In my husband's case, the pastors of our church supported us in prayer, taking authority over the spirits of rejection and anger that held him captive. Luis experienced spiritual freedom that gave him the power to relinquish his need for obsessive order. His inner world had been in disorder, and he had been seeking peace by trying to order his outer world. Luis found freedom that night, and since then he has had the ability to control his emotions. He still faces the temptation of failing in that area, but he is now free to choose to walk in the Spirit rather than the flesh.

In Christ we are called to set captives free and heal the wounded:

> The Spirit of the Sovereign Lord is on me,
> because the Lord has anointed me
> to proclaim good news to the poor.
> He has sent me to bind up the brokenhearted,
> to proclaim freedom for the captives
> and release from darkness for the prisoners
>
> (Isaiah 61:1).

This Bible passage is talking about the ministry of Jesus, but we know God has called us to the same ministry. What better place to do this than in our home, starting with our marriage! Our journey through this world is difficult, and we are all broken in some way. If we had spiritual x-ray vision, then instead of seeing a glamorous bride and handsome groom on our wedding day, we would see two people injured and bandaged, perhaps in wheelchairs or on crutches. We need to understand that God gives us the opportunity to be His hands and heal our spouse. Rather than viewing their weaknesses as something intentional they do to upset us, we should realize something is broken in their life, and we have an opportunity to be part of their healing. The perspective and attitude we choose will make all the difference.

It's exciting to think that God has given us the amazing gift of free will. With that gift comes the ability to choose. We can choose to love God and love others. We can choose to change and not continue in the same harmful patterns. We can choose to see our differences as our strengths and reach our full potential as a couple, reflecting a more complete picture of our amazing God!

CHAPTER 4

The Secret **to Intimacy**

*This explains why a man leaves his father
and mother and is joined to his wife,
and the two are united into one.*
—Genesis 2:24 (NLT)

WHEN WE HEAR "INTIMACY IN MARRIAGE," MOST OF us immediately think of sex. And it's true—God created sex as part of intimacy.

> A man . . . is joined to his wife, and the two are united into one. Now the man and his wife were both naked, but they felt no shame (Genesis 2:24-25 NLT).

These verses are definitely talking about sex, but they also point toward emotional and spiritual nakedness—the complete intimacy of body, soul, and spirit. Taking off your clothes and being physically naked may come easy for some people, but it requires even more confidence to remove the mask of the soul and be known for who you really are. Luis and I have been in many counseling sessions in which we hear complaints of dissatisfaction in sexual intimacy. But it doesn't compare to the number of couples we've met who struggle with dissatisfaction in emotional intimacy. Many times, they do not have the words to express that feeling. We hear phrases such as:

- "I feel disconnected."
- "We live in two different worlds."
- "I feel like she doesn't understand me."
- "I have no idea how he feels."
- "I'm not asking for a solution; I just want him to listen to me."
- "I feel like she doesn't really know me."
- "When the children leave, I'm afraid we won't have anything in common."

The same disconnect can happen with spiritual intimacy:

- "We never pray together."
- "I feel embarrassed to tell her what I am feeling from God."
- "I would like to read the Bible with him, but it never happens."
- "I feel judged when I pray in front of him."
- "I feel that she expects too much of me in this area."

These are all expressions of dissatisfaction with the level of intimacy. The good news is that we can grow in every area of our marital intimacy—spiritual, emotional, and sexual.

The key to improving in any of these areas is not to settle for less. God created us to have deep intimacy with Him and with our spouse; He programmed it into our DNA in the Garden. But we tend to settle for only one or the other. If we have a satisfying relationship with our spouse, we may rely on the security of our marriage and neglect our relationship with God. Or if we have a satisfying relationship with God, we might neglect our marital relationship and rely solely on Him. God's plan from the beginning was for us to experience intimacy in both relationships. We are not going to feel complete if we settle for less. There is a beautiful worship song with the chorus "All I ever need is You," and it is about needing only God in our lives. The lyrics are poetic and inspiring, but they are only partly true. While it is true that only God's love fills us completely, He created us to need people, and He chooses to express His love to us through those people. Yes, even broken, very imperfect people! Not all of us are blessed to have strong relationships that show us His *agape* love. When people fail us, or we have experienced the loss of a loved one, God in His mercy fills those holes in our hearts. Relational loss affects us so deeply because we were created for intimate relationships. God created us to know and be known. Our greatest satisfaction in marriage comes from growing in deeper intimacy with our spouse spiritually, emotionally, and physically.

I want all three of things with you.

Spiritual Intimacy

In the Garden of Eden, Adam walked with God and talked with Him face to face. God gave Adam the task of taking care of the garden and then said, "It is not good for the man to be alone. I will make a helper who is just right for him"

(Genesis 2:18 NLT). The incredible thing about this passage is that man was not alone—God was with him. God loved Adam, but He knew His creation needed to experience that love with his five senses. So God created the ideal helper for him. The King James Version uses the term "help meet." The word help in this passage comes from the Hebrew word *ezer*, and it is amazing that God uses this word to refer to Himself in Psalm 33:20: "We put our hope in the LORD. He is our help [*ezer*] and our shield" (NLT). God's message to us in calling the woman *ezer* is beautiful. He was saying to Adam, "Just as I breathed My breath into you, I am depositing part of My essence in her, because I know you need to feel My love with the same hands you have. You need to hear My words of encouragement with the same lips you have, and you need to know that I am with you every time you feel her by your side."

[Handwritten margin note: Wow, that's beautiful ♡]

Isn't our God amazing?! His plan was perfect, and all was well until sin broke the connection of intimacy between God and humanity and between the man and woman. The good news is the connection has been restored through the sacrifice of Jesus. And not only was it restored, but it also received an upgrade. In Christ we can experience Intimacy 2.0, augmented and improved! The veil was torn, and we now have direct access to the love of the Father. And the most incredible thing is God gives us the privilege of presenting that divine love to the world through our marriage:

> "For this reason a man will leave his father and mother and be united to his wife, and the two will become one flesh." This is a profound mystery—but I am talking about Christ and the church. However, each one of you also must love his wife as he loves himself, and the wife must respect her husband (Ephesians 5:31–33).

"This is a profound mystery." We might think that a mystery is a big secret, something we will never understand, but this is not the case for the children of God. The Greek word for mystery is *musterion*. In Mark 4:11, Jesus tells His disciples, "You are allowed to understand the secret [*musterion*] of the kingdom of God; but I use parables to speak to outsiders" (NLT). When we see *musterion* in the Bible, it does not refer to something that cannot be known but rather to something that can only be known with God's revelation.[7] God's desire is to give us revelation so that we can live the truth of this passage. But it requires humility. There is always more revelation available when we are willing to take the time and humbly ask Him. Take a moment now and ask the Holy Spirit for more revelation about being one just like Christ and His Church.

> Holy Spirit, open my mind and heart to have revelation about how You view my marriage and how we can have deeper intimacy. Our desire is to be a testimony of Your love to the world around us. I ask this in Jesus' name, Amen.

Prayer is the key to experiencing more spiritual intimacy. It should come as no surprise that most Christian couples have a hard time praying together, because there is so much spiritual resistance around it. I'm not talking about simple prayers, like blessing the food or asking for good dreams at bedtime. Those are a start, but they aren't the kind of prayers that will unite your hearts with the heart of God regarding the needs of your family. To set aside time to pray,

---

[7] Joseph Thayer, *Thayer's Greek-English Lexicon of the New Testament*, s.v. "musterion," American Book Company, 2020, Kindle, 2360–2362.

you will have to fight against evil spiritual forces and the natural stream of distractions, exhaustion, and entertainment that is always competing for our attention. It is not easy, but the payoff in your marriage will be worth it.

Another way to connect spiritually is to set aside time to share what you have read in the Bible and the revelation you have received in your quiet time. Just make sure the effort to improve in these areas does not turn into a conflict. Normally, there is one person who is more willing than the other. No one should feel forced to pray or open their heart. Obviously, that defeats the purpose. It is important to express your desire to grow in your spiritual connection and to be proactive in suggesting it, but if your spouse shows resistance, don't push it. It is better to ask God to move on your spouse's heart.

One of the questions we often get is what to do when someone in the relationship is not a believer or is not interested in spiritual things. I believe this is one of the main reasons why Paul said we should not be unequally yoked (2 Corinthians 6:14). When we join our life with a person who does not have a renewed spirit, there is a limit on the intimacy we can experience together. If you are already married, then the best thing you can do is pray against the evil spirits that have blinded your spouse from seeing the light of Christ (2 Corinthians 4:4). The Bible also tells us that showing God's grace and treating them with love and respect can break their resistance to the gospel (1 Peter 3:1–2). It is not an easy task, but there is nothing impossible for God!

Emotional Intimacy

Emotional connection is essential for a relationship to flourish and last. Sometimes we look down on emotions and see them as negative: "I can't talk to you because you're so emotional. We need to be more rational, not emotional." Men especially tend to struggle in this area. Of course, it is not because they do not feel. Men feel deeply as do women. But sometimes because of family culture or their personality, they lack the emotional vocabulary to share their most vulnerable feelings. For many men it is easy to say, "I'm upset, tired, fed up..." It is much more difficult to express, "I have fears," "I need you," "It hurts when..." etc.

Expressions of vulnerability are essential for experiencing true intimacy. It is important to mention here that although our emotions are vital for intimacy, they should never control us. Like most couples, if Luis and I made our decisions based solely on emotions, we would definitely not be together today! I very much agree with the saying, "Love is not a feeling; it is a commitment," but we should not discount emotions from our experience. They are gifts from God and necessary to experience wholeness in any relationship. God Himself is emotional. The Bible tells us about His love, laughter, compassion, sadness, anger, jealousy, joy, and so on. The key to having healthy emotional connections is to submit them to the authority of the Holy Spirit. If we don't, then they can betray us. Emotions were made to follow our will, not our will to follow our emotions.

There are false emotions that can seem so real, but they are not our true feelings. In a moment of anger, we can unleash a barrage of insults and then later regret it. I call them counterfeit emotions. They are shoddy and distorted copies of true emotions. In the moment, it seems easy and "cheap" to let them loose, but the end result is costly. As the Mexican adage goes, "Lo barato sale caro." ("Cheap things end up being expensive.") When we first moved to Mexico, we rented an apartment near a *tianguis* (an open-air market). I loved walking through the crowded aisles filled with colorful clothing, trinkets, and culinary aromas. One day I discovered a stand that sold movies (in those days we had VHS tapes), and I was amazed because they were so cheap. I love a good deal, so with great excitement, I bought several videos for the children. When I got home, Luis quickly burst my bubble by explaining that they were pirated. They were cheap copies made illegally.

I soon learned that not only were the movies illegal contraband, but they were also very poor quality! I ended up throwing them all away. Now I understand the commercials I kept seeing on television: "Say no to piracy!" That is the same attitude we should take with our emotional health—"Say no to false emotions!" It is easy to think and say things that are not what you truly feel, but it's also costly. If you keep thinking and speaking them, then they can become your true emotions. A divorce does not happen overnight. It is an accumulation of uncontrolled emotions and poorly made decisions. Emotional self-control is key to creating lasting bonds of connection. When we successfully create these bonds, our marriage flourishes and is able to withstand the storms of life.

There is an important concept in the subject of emotional intimacy that is called attachment. In the mid 1900s, psychoanalyst John Bowlby dedicated himself to studying the emotional ties that are created in childhood between children and their adult caregivers. The result of his studies showed that attachment (the psychological bond of connection between human beings) is vital for survival and healthy development. Physical sustenance alone is not enough. Bowlby opened the way for further studies focusing on adults, and to no surprise, he discovered that it is not only children who need emotional attachment to thrive but also adults. Of course, the same is true for marriage. We cannot thrive together without healthy and secure emotional attachment. (I recommend the book *Created for Connection* by Dr. Sue Johnson and Kenneth Sanderfer on this subject.)[8]

Secure attachment takes place when the child or adult knows the other person will attend to their needs, give emotional support, and provide protection. The person then feels secure and can make healthy and lasting interpersonal connections. To open up emotionally, we need to feel safe and secure. We have to be intentional in creating that safe place, starting with an honest evaluation: *How are we doing now?* If you buy a security system for your home, the first thing the company is going to do is assess how secure your home is at the moment. They will identify the most vulnerable areas and what is most needed. It is the same in your marriage. Start off with a good conversation, using questions designed to reveal the health of your emotional connections. Some key questions include:

- "Can you count on me to listen and respond to your needs?"
- "Am I accessible to and open with you?"
- "Do I respond to you with my heart (emotions) and not only with my mind (solutions)?"

---

8. Susan M. Johnson and Kenneth Sanderfer, *Created for Connection: The "HOLD Me Tight" Guide for Christian Couples* (New York, NY: Hachette Book Group Incorporated, 2016).

- "Do I value and appreciate your feelings?"
- "Am I loyal?"
- "Do you know you can trust me?"
- "Even in the middle of the conflict, do you know I still love you?"

The inability to answer "Yes" to those questions causes emotional insecurity. We feel unprotected and in danger. What happens when we sense danger? Our reaction is fight, flight, or freeze. These physical responses are programmed into our DNA to help us survive, but they definitely don't help us create healthy relationships! These same physiological reactions also happen psychologically when we feel emotionally unsafe. When we sense that our attachment and connection have been broken, an alarm sounds within us. Sadly, none of the "natural" responses are helpful. There are people who react immediately with a fight response. Preparing to defend themselves, they raise their voices and put on a show of strength to intimidate their spouse and stay "safe." If the lack of attachment continues, they are left with feelings of anger and frustration. Those who react by fleeing stop talking and prefer to leave the room. They distract themselves with activities to avoid the problem. If the lack of attachment continues, they are left emotionally disconnected and absent. Those who freeze feel emotionally paralyzed. They can't think clearly or respond, so they are left speechless. If attachment is not restored, they struggle with emotional numbness and have a hard time functioning or being productive. None of these survival responses fix the problem; on the contrary, they only cause more damage. These are natural reactions, but God gives us the ability to react supernaturally. With the help of the Holy Spirit, we can stop the harmful cycle and move beyond instinctive reactions.

The root of most conflict is a lack of secure attachment, so the most effective solution is to restore a sense of protection and emotional connection. Many times, we treat the symptoms rather than the disease. We say things like, "We need to talk. It is not good to be silent," or "It is not healthy to shout and fight; I'm not going to do it anymore." That can help relieve symptoms, but it doesn't cure the problem unless you first restore a safe emotional environment. Go back to the key questions and ask yourself how you can better show your spouse that he or she can count on you, how you can be more emotionally accessible, etc. Those are excellent starting points for not only discussing them as a couple but also with God. Many times, we are blind to our weak areas, and we need the Holy Spirit to shine His light on our hearts. We can also have broken areas in our emotions that only God can heal. There is a well-known (not Mexican!) saying: "Hurt people hurt people." The good news is the other side of the coin: Free people free people! The best way to walk in emotional freedom together is to be intentional. Decide today to submit your emotions to the authority of God and be intentional in bonding emotionally with your spouse.

Physical Intimacy

(And all the men cheer, "Yes! Finally we get to the good stuff!") It's true—sex is good and such an important part of physical intimacy. But before we go there, we want to talk about another part that is equally important: non-sexual touch. (And now all the women cheer!) It's no secret that men and women approach physical intimacy differently.

As we mentioned in the previous chapter, a basic need of women is non-sexual affection, and a basic need of men is sexual affection. The most incredible thing is that both are necessary to create secure and lasting bonds of intimacy. God doesn't make mistakes. He is a master designer. Being so different is actually the perfect plan to magnify the intimacy we experience. It may not come naturally for some people, but it is so important to be intentional about making small physical connections throughout the day. Be intentional in holding hands, hugging, sitting close, rubbing his shoulders, caressing her hair, etc. There are many sociological and psychological studies that show the power of physical touch and its role in creating secure attachment. From birth to old age, we are created to give and receive affection through touch, and the benefits go beyond the psychological and emotional. Studies show that affectionate touch increases serotonin and oxytocin levels (hormones that give us a feeling of peace and well-being), lowers heart rate, lowers blood pressure, and improves the immune system.[9] Wow, what an incredible gift from God! And in marriage we are blessed to experience the benefits of physical touch in a deeper way through sexual touch.

Sex is one of the areas that can be complicated to navigate because it feels so vulnerable. Talking about our sexual relationship with each other can be uncomfortable. Getting help and talking about it with someone else is even more uncomfortable. What complicates it even further is the fact that our society is hypersexual. If you watch a lot of television, you will think your love life is a total failure if you don't have constant,

---

9. Danielle Friedman, "The One Thing Happy Couples Do Every Day To Keep Their Relationship Strong," Health.com, February 13, 2018, https://www.health.com/relationships/benefits-touch-your-partner-every-day.

passionate sex. Sadly, this amazing gift of God, created to unite us, can become an idol of pleasure or pain that divides us. There are so many factors that can muddy the waters when it comes to bringing up the subject: insecurities, fear of rejection, lack of knowledge, doubts, sinful influences, bad advice, addictions, abuse, sickness ... and the list goes on.

But the good news is God is the Creator of sex and marriage. He has the answer to whatever challenges we face in this area. The best sex is sex under the design and blessing of God; we can call it divine sex. The enemy lies to us that the best sex is forbidden, perverse, and secret. Satan is not the creator of anything. He can only pervert and distort what God creates. A cheap, distorted copy is never going to be as beautiful as the original artwork. If you feel like your sex life looks nothing like a divine work of art, I have good news for you. God has an uncanny ability to take what is complicated and broken, what seems to have no solution, and make it beautiful with the whisper of His voice. Our desire is for you to hear the voice of the Creator speaking over your sexuality, bringing revelation, healing, and freedom! The best place to start hearing His voice is through the Bible, the inspired Word of God.

We will start with five basic questions (who, how, where, when, and why) and see how the Scriptures answer them regarding divine sex, beautiful and blessed by God.

Who?

> Give honor to marriage, and remain faithful to one another in marriage. God will surely judge people who are immoral and those who commit adultery (Hebrews 13:4 NLT).

"Haven't you read," he replied, "that at the beginning the Creator 'made them male and female,' and said, 'For this reason a man will leave his father and mother and be united to his wife, and the two will become one flesh' (Matthew 19:4–5).

It is clear in the Bible that divine sex is between a man and a woman in the sanctity of marriage. It does not include other people, physically or virtually. This is why pornography is so harmful; it is like committing virtual infidelity, and it invokes God's judgment according to Hebrews 13:4.

How?

The word faithful in Hebrews 13:4 is the Greek word *amiantos*, which has a very interesting meaning in relation to sex. It is defined as "not defiled, unsoiled; free from that by which the nature of a thing is deformed and debased, or its force and vigor impaired."[10] It is a beautiful description of purity.

We have to keep our sexual relationship pure. What is important to understand is that purity in practice can be interpreted differently for each couple. There are clear parameters in the Bible, like faithfulness mentioned in the previous point. But there are other parameters that are not so clear. We are often asked in premarital counseling, "What can we do or not do?" What they are asking is, "Are there sexual practices that are not allowed in a Christian marriage?" I feel that Paul's instructions in 1 Corinthians 10:23–24 are very relevant on this subject:

---

10. Joseph Thayer, s.v. "amiantos," 748.

"I have the right to do anything," you say—but not everything is beneficial. "I have the right to do anything"—but not everything is constructive. No one should seek their own good, but the good of others.

The key is for the two of you to agree and have peace about it.

There is sexual activity, like oral sex for example, that one could say is mentioned (indirectly) in the book of Song of Solomon in the Bible as an expression of pure love and pleasure. For some couples, this is an enjoyable experience. But for others, that kind of sexual activity may be uncomfortable. It is better to avoid anything that brings feelings of condemnation or is not mutually enjoyed.

There are some key questions we recommend considering before naming a sexual act pure:

- Is it forbidden in the Bible?
- Is it unnatural (against God's natural design)?
- Can it cause physical harm?
- Is it loving and not obligated?
- Do the two of you agree in good conscience?

Where?

In the kitchen. No, it is not what you are thinking! Sexual intimacy begins at breakfast and continues all day—an affectionate word, a gesture of consideration by helping to wash the dishes, a short love note, a playful text. Every moment of thoughtfulness helps to create bonds of affection that can culminate in an exciting night in the bedroom. But remember, that isn't the goal. Enjoy the affection for what it is, not where it might lead. Women especially tend to be guarded and resistant if they think their husbands are only being sweet because they want something more. It is important to remember that intimacy is the end goal, and it is created throughout the whole day.

When?

> Do not deprive each other except perhaps by mutual consent and for a time, so that you may devote yourselves to prayer. Then come together again so that Satan will not tempt you because of your lack of self-control (1 Corinthians 7:5).

It is no secret that most couples have disproportionate libidos (sexual drives). It is so common that it has a clinical name: sexual desire discrepancy (SDD). That difference can turn into an ongoing conflict or an opportunity to love our spouse even when it is not our own need. That is called *agape* love. The frequency of our sexual encounters depends on many factors: the libido of each person, the stage of life (pregnancy, having young children, menopause, andropause), the level of emotional attachment, general health, work hours, etc. The important thing is that the two of you are in agreement with your sexual frequency and that you have some kind of regularity. When you go too long without sex, the level of your emotional connection and intimacy in general suffers. There is a fascinating study that measured couples' happiness related to the frequency of sexual activity. Interestingly, happiness peaked with one sexual encounter per week.[11] That means that couples who had sex at least once a week experienced more happiness in their relationship than those who had less sex, but they experienced the same level of happiness as those who had more frequent sexual encounters. Obviously, being sexually intimate once a week is not a formula for happiness. (I wish it were that simple!) For some people it would be a lot and for others too little, but it clearly shows the connection between a sense of happiness and well-being in marriage and consistent and frequent sexual intimacy.

Why?

Let's look again at Matthew 19:5: "This explains why a man leaves his father and mother and is joined to his wife, and the two are united into one" (NLT). We always have to keep the why in mind, no matter what we do. We will never reach the goal if we don't know what it is. The ultimate goal of sexual intimacy is oneness, not the experience itself. It is a path to a destination, not *the* destination. Anything besides God that is the center of our attention can be an idol. Sex is no exception. In our modern culture it has become an idol, and the same can be true in our marriage.

When sex takes center stage, it tends to cause a tremendous amount of conflict. We knew a couple who sadly divorced, and one of the reasons was that she was obsessed with sex. No, that was not a typo—I said *she*, not he! The woman viewed sex recreationally, as a way to relieve stress.

---

11. Amy Muise, Ulrich Schimmack, and Emily A. Impett, "Sexual Frequency Predicts Greater Well-Being, But More Is Not Always Better," *Social Psychological and Personality Science* 7, no. 4 (May 2016): 295–302. https://doi.org/10.1177/1948550615616462.

Her high libido could have been a blessing in their marriage. However, the problem was that her husband began to feel pressured and objectified. He felt unable to please her in other areas of the marriage (she was highly critical of him in general), and he lost his desire to please her sexually. This is more common the other way, with demanding and critical men who have high libidos and make their wives feel like sexual objects. There is sex but no intimacy. We knew another couple who told us that for 20 years they had sex almost every day. It was part of their daily routine, like brushing their teeth and taking out the trash. But just like the other couple, they lacked intimacy in other areas of the relationship, and the marriage sadly ended in divorce. We can't forget the "why"!

Sex doesn't always have to be a euphoric connection. We should never feel pressured by how it "should" be. There are different ways to enjoy sexual intimacy, just as there are different ways to enjoy food. There is fine dining, fast food, health food, savory snacks, and rich desserts. Sex in a long-term committed relationship is also like that. There are times when it's a lot like fine dining. You take the time to make a reservation, notice the small details, and care about enjoying each moment. Other times, it's just a quickie, like going through the drive-through at McDonald's. It serves the purpose when you don't have the time or energy for something better! There are also encounters that feel like eating health food. You're not really in the mood for it, but you do it because you know it's good for you. And there are always those times like snacks, when you eat because it's fun and recreational. Let's not forget the desserts, those sweet endings after a long day. Variety is what makes life interesting.

There may be people reading this who are thinking, *That all sounds good, but that is not my experience. For me, sex* is more like rotten food. It causes more harm than good. It causes so many arguments and conflicts that it leaves a bad taste in my mouth. Or it could be that you feel like you're starving to death because you live in a marriage without sex. You are not alone. In fact, according to studies, approximately 15 percent of today's marriages are either sexless or have sex less than 10 times a year.[12] Sadly, that percentage has risen in recent years. An interesting fact is that researchers believe the rise correlates with the increase of cell phone usage and access to social media. I would also add the easy access to pornography. We have seen and talked to other pastors who are seeing more and more cases of young married couples struggling with dysfunctional sex lives due to the damage incurred by pornography. Lustful habits that started when they were single, thinking that everything would be cured by getting married, continued, and the consequences were devastating. I'm talking about Christian young people who have the best intentions of having a good, God-honoring marriage. By opening the door to the enemy in the area of their sexuality, they now find themselves trapped. And sadly, their spouse pays the consequences as well.

Whatever the reason may be for not having a satisfying sex life, there is always hope. Pray about it and get help. Ask the Lord to reveal the root of the problem. It could be a spiritual, emotional, or physical problem. Good communication is key to finding freedom in this area. Talk to your spouse, find a time when you both are relaxed (not during a sexual moment since it's too vulnerable), and ask for their help. Agree to find help together because sexual dissatisfaction

---

12. Elena Donovan Mauer, "Are Sexless Marriages More Common than We Think?," The Healthy, March 2, 2021, https://www.thehealthy.com/family/relationships/are-sexless-marriages-more-common-than-we-think/.

affects both of you. It may be wise to seek professional advice. There are so many factors that can affect this area, such as childhood abuse, negative experiences, ignorance, selfishness, addictions, health problems, etc. The important thing is not to suffer in silence. God's desire is for you to enjoy a full and satisfying sexual relationship.

If you are feeling sexual rejection from your spouse, it's so important to resist anger and frustration and try to focus on being part of the solution. It is important to take your spouse's side and face the problem together in unity. Even if you feel offended, remember that they are not the enemy. They are a victim just like you. There is a very real enemy who wants to rob both of you of the beauty of sexual pleasure. If you suffer from low libido (aside from seeking spiritual, emotional, or physical healing if necessary), remember that good sex is not simply something physical. Where is the most stimulating pleasure center in the body? It is in the brain! Use your thoughts to your advantage. Tell yourself a good story. The body responds to the internal story that you are telling. Instead of thinking about everything that bothers you about your spouse, think about everything that attracts you. Remember those romantic moments when you were dating. The imagination is a powerful tool. The enemy has tried to confiscate it, using it to his full advantage in the porn industry and also with romance novels. But the imagination is a gift from God. We need to rescue it and use it, imagining a pure and passionate sexual relationship with our spouse.

Great sex is not the end goal; it's only part of the journey toward creating bonds of secure attachment. Intimacy is a gift from God, uniting not only our bodies but also our hearts. The secret of intimacy is being intentional in being one. Each area of intimacy is linked to the others. We must be diligent in taking care of the spiritual, emotional, and physical connections in our relationship. Everything good in this world costs something; nothing gets better on its own. It requires time and effort. Be encouraged. No matter where you find yourselves on the road to more intimacy, it is worth the sacrifice to go deeper. Whoever travels there finds what we all long for—intimate connection with the one who holds our heart.

CHAPTER 5

Communication **Keys**

Whoever believes in me, as Scripture has said, rivers of living water will flow from within them.
—JOHN 7:38

OUR WORDS SHOULD BE LIKE REFRESHING WATER, giving life to those who listen. But when we are not careful with what we say, our words are like bitter tonic. We could save ourselves a lot of conflict in our marriage if we chose to communicate better. Raising our voice, using sarcasm, ridiculing, "thinking out loud," and saying what we don't mean causes unnecessary stress and pain. An incredible amount of hurt could be avoided if we simply communicated differently. One thoughtless, angry word can damage someone's heart forever. It only takes a second to say but a lifetime to regret.

God warns us in His Word that the power of life and death is in the tongue (Proverbs 18:21). The frustrations and bitterness in our hearts spill out of our mouths faster than we can contain them. "Out of the abundance of the heart the mouth speaks" (Matthew 12:34 NKJV). What a profound truth! Sometimes we say, "I didn't mean that," but the problem is that by not having self-control and saying the first thing that comes to mind, we develop a bad habit. At some point what we say is going to connect with our heart. When this happens, we believe what we said. What we did not mean before, we now do. And in that moment our words carry power.

By continually speaking negative words, we run the risk that they will connect with our heart and come to life. You've probably heard things like, "I know it's not true, but what they said hurt me deeply." Well, if you know it's not true, then why did it hurt? It hurt because those words made a connection with your heart. They bypassed your mind's reason and caused pain because your heart believed them. The same is true for the one speaking. You might think it's not what you really mean, but imagine your heart is like a water reservoir. Water is stored there, either clean or polluted. Now imagine your mouth as the spout. Although you say it was not your intention to offend or hurt, where did the polluted water come from? From the reservoir in your heart.

If we truly understand this, we will be more careful with what we are allowing both in and out of our heart. Communication is key in marriage. We know this. We have heard it, read it, and shared it repeatedly, but still we let our emotions control our tongue. The good news is there is a solution. Remember that we are talking about a divine marriage in which God is the center. When we receive Jesus as our Lord and Savior, we receive the power of the Holy Spirit and the ability to change. He cleans up the reservoir, replacing the toxic, putrid water with perfect living water. It's then our job to steward that deposit and keep it clean. Jesus tells us to be careful of what enters our mind because it affects our heart. The way to control what enters our mind is to control what we see, hear, and read. It might seem like this has nothing to do with our communication, but what is in our heart is what will come out of our mouth.

We cannot give what we do not have. If we are having a difficult time showing love, compassion, grace, and mercy, it's an indication that we have a heart problem. Our words are like a heart monitor. They alert us to problems we can't see on the surface. If our words are continually harsh, then we are probably struggling with bitterness. Something has contaminated the water, and sooner or later it comes spewing out of our mouths. Good communication starts with a clean heart:

> Search me, O God, and know my heart;
> test me and know my anxious thoughts.
> Point out anything in me that offends you,
> and lead me along the path of everlasting life
> (Psalm 139:23–24 NLT).

The beauty of a divine marriage is that the Holy Spirit helps us change the way we communicate by changing our heart. Try asking Him for help. "Create in me a clean heart, O God; and renew a right spirit within me" (Psalm 51:10 KJV).

In our almost 30 years of marriage, Kristen and I have had many beautiful moments and other not-so-beautiful moments. We have opened our hearts and shared the deepest parts of who we are. We have laughed, cried, and argued. Touching the deepest fibers of the soul isn't easy, and it requires trust. I (Luis) think we have been surprised by how difficult it has been at times for us to communicate correctly. Even at this point in our marriage we still have misunderstandings and sometimes struggle with being patient and kind in the way we talk to each other. We still need our hearts to be healed and restored through the work of the Holy Spirit. I acknowledge that I still sometimes have a hard time controlling my thoughts and reactions when Kristen pushes my buttons, exposing my insecurities and pride. But we've discovered forgiveness and the way back to each other. The Holy Spirit offers us a path to deliverance, healing, and restoration. We have traveled there many times. Every time we have a conflict and offend each other due to bad communication, we can hear the Holy Spirit speaking to our thoughts: "You have to go back and ask for forgiveness. Do not go to bed with resentment and anger in your heart." Ephesians 4:26 says, "'Don't sin by letting anger control you.' Don't let the sun go down while you are still angry" (NLT).

We have forgiven many times and seen the fruit of restoration. But in other instances we have decided to hold on to our pride and pay the costly consequences. On one occasion, Kristen and I were celebrating our anniversary, and I invited her to breakfast. While driving there, one of those topics came up that should not be touched on an anniversary. Kristen, in my opinion, kept pushing on it, and I started to lose self-control. We got to the restaurant a bit upset, and things went downhill from there. I had planned to surprise her with a ring I had resized. She had put it away years ago, waiting for us to have enough money to send it to a jeweler. I was excited to surprise her, and my plan was to pick it up at the jewelry store after breakfast. But on the way from the restaurant to the store, things went from bad to worse, and by the time we arrived, I had a terrible attitude. We were about to walk into the store when I said to Kristen, "You know what? I don't want to do this. Let's go." She insisted on not leaving, and that made me even angrier. I stormed back to the car alone. Slamming the door behind me, I felt the Holy Spirit say, "Stop!" But I completely ignored His warning and accelerated in reverse. At that moment, a car was also backing out from the spot right behind me (what a coincidence), and we collided. It was a pretty strong impact because I had pulled out so fast. I sat in the car in shock. What happened? I lost control, and someone else took it. And that someone was not on my side. I let the devil poison my heart toward my wife whom I love, and I used horrible words to lash out at her. (Just remembering that day makes me want to cry all over again.)

As you can imagine, things did not end that day as planned. We finally picked up the ring after the hassle of the insurance claim. We were able to ask for forgiveness and pray together but then spent the rest of the day in silence. It cost a good deal of money, time, and effort to fix all the damage not only to our car but also to our relationship. I lost several years of growth in my relationship with God and with Kristen. All because of pride. But I was truly repentant, and although there were consequences, we experienced the grace of God. It would have been so much better had I chosen not to argue and instead drawn living water from my heart, but what came out was far from life giving. Sadly, I lost that battle, but thank God, I did not lose the war against our marriage! Thank God for the path of forgiveness. First John 1:9 says, "If we confess our sins, he is faithful and just and will forgive us our sins and purify us from all unrighteousness." James 5:16 says, "Therefore confess your sins to each other, and pray for each other so that you may be healed. The prayer of a righteous person is powerful and effective." Kristen and I have deeply hurt each other over the years. If it wasn't for the divine guidance of the Holy Spirit leading us to forgive, we would not be writing this book today.

People might see us and think, *What a beautiful couple. Surely, they don't have any problems. They seem perfect together.* The truth is, we have conflicts like any marriage, and they are usually about small and insignificant things. What has made the difference in our communication is that we have walked the path of forgiveness. God has taught us to resolve our conflicts quickly. Communication is not only the words we speak—it's also the heart behind them. Divine communication is being willing to submit our hearts, thoughts, and words to God. It is not a matter of just wanting things to get better but instead obeying and making steps toward change. When you feel God telling you to ask for forgiveness or to forgive, you have the opportunity to take the attitude of Jesus and humble yourself. Jesus said: "Learn from me, for I am gentle and humble in heart" (Matthew 11:29).

We have gone through different stages of maturity in communication in our marriage, and we want to encourage you to view divine communication in your marriage as a process. It will take time to build trust and be able to connect deeply. But we assure you that if you stay persistent and continually invite the Lord Jesus to guide you to communicate and understand each other better, you will.

At different times I have had to go and kneel before God and pray: "Father, I don't understand her. Help me see Kristen as You see her. Show me Your heart toward her. Holy Spirit, guide me in my communication with her." And I'm sure she has done this too. What do you think happens? In some cases, things are resolved quickly, but other times it is a process. I have to take the time to be intentional in communicating better. I have learned over time that it is better to listen than to speak. As my mother would say, "Calladita me veo mas bonita!" ("I am better looking with my mouth shut!") I have made it a personal goal to grow in the different levels of communication, because each one is important to have deeper connection. These levels include:

- casual communication
- intentional communication
- emotional communication
- spiritual communication

Casual Communication

This is what we use to talk about the ins and outs of daily life: "Good morning. The coffee is ready. I am going to take the children to school. See you for dinner. Don't forget we have Danny's ball game tonight. You look good today, honey. Remember to pick up milk on your way home. So what time are you coming back today? Do you want to have something for breakfast? Do you think we can go see my mom this weekend? What time are we leaving for church?" Without this type of communication, we could not even have a cordial relationship. This is the most basic communication in marriage. It is what helps us coordinate our lives and create basic connections. Casual communication does not take much time or effort, but sadly there are couples who cannot communicate well with love and respect even at this level. Instead, they experience rejection, loneliness, and misunderstandings. The key to good casual communication is not only being aware of what we say but also how we say it.

> A gentle answer turns away wrath,
> but a harsh word stirs up anger
> (Proverbs 15:1).

Intentional Communication

This level includes sharing our thoughts and getting feedback on something in particular:

- "You know, I was thinking we should plan some time away."
- "Why don't we take some time to talk more about what happened last night?"
- "I want to hear what you think about Heather's situation."
- "I think we need to revisit the budget."
- "We need to make a decision about John's school this week."

This type of communication does not happen if we do not make dedicated time to talk about the issues that will determine the direction of the week, the month, or the following years. It involves topics such as living arrangements, money management, beliefs and customs, children, schools, jobs, vacations, church ... basically anything related to the managing of our lives. Without this type of communication, it is very difficult to have clear direction. Kristen and I have many conversations about these issues, and it helps us stay unified through the twists and turns of life. We also know that without God's intervention, it can be challenging to agree on important issues. We can't always get past our differences of opinion, so we invite the Holy Spirit to be the tie breaker!

In some situations, it is difficult to know the right thing to do. Only the Lord can guide us, for only He holds the future in His hands. Taking time to pray and seek His Word regarding the issue helps us make those hard decisions. It is not always easy, because we can confuse our own will with God's will. Kristen has told me more than once, "I am not sure I trust you on this one, but I trust God, and no matter what happens, He will help us through it." When we are facing challenging decisions together, I hold on to Psalm 46:10: "Be still, and know that I am God." When we decide to stay still for a moment, a week, a month, or even years and do nothing until we feel the peace of Jesus, then things work out in our favor. When we rush (as I am prone to do), things don't go as smoothly as they could (see Proverbs 14:16). Waiting on the Lord takes self-control, which is a fruit of the Holy Spirit (Galatians 5:22-23). If this is difficult for you, like it is for me, ask the Lord for more of His Spirit in your life. We need to purposefully plan these conversations so that we don't float aimlessly through life and miss out on experiencing great opportunities while avoiding the negative ones. Intentionality is key.

Emotional Communication

This type of communication leads us to an even deeper connection. Men often feel that we are having emotional conversations with our wives when we discuss important topics such as the ones described above. But I have learned that intentional communication is very different from emotional communication. Emotional communication, as the word says, has to do with emotions—feelings. For men, these are usually the most difficult conversations to navigate. We hardly ever make time for them because we fear things might unravel if we do. They open doors to the depths of the heart, to feelings that many times we do not even know are there.

In our experience, it can take years to get into these back rooms of our souls. We have worked hard to get to where we are today in this area.

Being married doesn't mean we know each other emotionally. God knows how deep and often deceptive the heart is. Talking about emotions is risky without a clear guide. Emotions are feelings that change with our circumstances; they are not necessarily 100 percent true. When we have these types of conversations, we should always speak in the first person ("I feel that...") with the perspective of finding the truth. Although we are being vulnerable and our feelings are very real in the moment, we can be fooled by our own heart: "The heart is deceitful above all things, and desperately wicked: who can know it?" (Jeremiah 17:9 NKJ). God warns us in this verse that we must be careful with our emotions, as they can betray us, creating ideas and stories that are often not true. (In the next chapter we will go into more detail on how to have emotional conversations specifically for conflict resolution.)

So why have these conversations at all? That is an excellent question. The answer is the benefits outweigh the risks. Sharing our dreams and passions and being known for who we really are is bonding. It is also healing and liberating. Jesus died to save us. The word save in Greek is *sozo*. It refers to being saved, healed, and delivered. It's a complete package of restoration—body, soul, and spirit. Opening our hearts and deeply knowing one another is part of *sozo*.

Emotional conversations are not about day-to-day decisions or planning. They have to do with our inner world—how we are really doing. Here are some questions that can serve as a guide for emotional conversations:

- What makes you feel at peace?
- Do you feel at peace in our marriage?
- What things rob your peace?
- What makes you feel fully alive?
- What are the dreams you have had that aren't completely fulfilled?
- How healthy are your friendships?
- Do you feel that you can open your heart to me without being judged, ridiculed, or belittled?
- What can I do to make you feel valued?
- Do you have doubts, questions, or insecurities about us?
- Can you identify painful areas in our relationship?
- What makes you feel truly whole when we are together?
- What makes you feel insecure and underappreciated when we are together?
- Is our intimate sexual relationship satisfying for you, or is there frustration in this area?
- Is there something you have wanted to share with me but haven't out of fear, rejection, or shame?
- How has our financial situation affected you, for better or for worse?
- Do you feel you can trust me?
- What are you willing to do to make a deeper connection as a couple?
- Are there unresolved emotional issues between us that affect our children?
- Are there unresolved issues with our children that affect our marriage?
- Do you agree with the way we are raising our children?
- Do you feel like we have open, honest conversations when we need to resolve problems?
- Are you willing to find help in the areas where we haven't been able to resolve our conflicts?

These are just examples to get you started. Feel free to add your own questions. Be patient and forgiving. Communicating at this level is exciting for some and terrifying for others. It takes maturity to do it well. It may even seem like it is creating more conflicts than connection, but it's most likely bringing what's already there to the surface. (Chapter 6 is dedicated entirely to step-by-step conflict resolution.) If you think you are not ready to communicate emotionally or have tried unsuccessfully, it may be a good idea to talk to a pastor, leader, marriage counselor, or someone with the ability to walk you through it. Don't give up without getting help. Vulnerability is never easy, but it's always worth it. Be realistic and don't expect everything to be settled in a couple of conversations. It takes time. We don't even fully understand our own emotions, but there is Someone who understands them perfectly. He is the Holy Spirit, and He can guide us to the next level, which is spiritual communication.

Spiritual Communication

Although the name sounds very serious and imposing, this is where we should feel the most comfortable as God's children. It simply means including the Holy Spirit in all the previous levels of communication. When the presence and ways of God are part of our conversations, they take us to a whole different place of intimacy—a place where there is rest instead of striving to change.

> Come to me, all you who are weary and burdened, and I will give you rest. Take my yoke upon you and learn from me, for I am gentle and humble in heart,

and you will find rest for your souls. For my yoke is easy and my burden is light (Matthew 11:28-30).

Pursuing a deeper relationship with our spouse should not feel like a burden. In reality, though, sometimes it does. God gives us the remedy: stop believing it depends on us. Bring Him our burdens, even the burden of being a better spouse. We were not designed to carry heavy burdens. We were made to bear only the Lord's burden, which is obedience. Anything He asks us to do is for our own benefit. If we truly trust Him, that burden is light.

Emotional conversations are meant to bring out what is nestled deep in our hearts. As God's children, it's not our job to fix what comes to the surface. Our heavenly Father has promised to complete the work He began in us (see Philippians 1:6). That's good news! When we have deep conversations together, we can bring them to the Lord, and He will give us everything we need. That is true freedom. Trusting that nothing is impossible for our Savior, we can turn to Him and say, "We don't know how to resolve these struggles, but You do."

We think when we open our hearts with our spouse, they should instantly understand us or have a solution. But many times, that is not the ultimate plan. God invites us to be part of the healing process, but only He is Jehovah Rapha, God our Healer. In my life, I struggled with a deep feeling of abandonment. When I was around 13 years old, I was kicked out of my house, and I experienced deep rejection from my parents, especially my father. I drifted around from one friend's house to another. When I ran out of options, I would spend nights on the street until another friend could take me in, sometimes hiding me in their garage or sneaking me through their bedroom window. I have tended to that wound many times, but there are moments when I am still sensitive about it. Kristen and I have talked and prayed, putting it before the Lord. I have opened up to other pastors who are part of my spiritual covering to help me fully heal. That type of abandonment does not heal with human love alone. Only God's perfect *agape* love can restore an orphaned heart. He speaks sonship over us, melting away the pain and rejection.

I have forgiven my father, but it has been a long healing process with many layers. There were times when I associated that abandonment with something Kristen said or did. I created stories in my mind that had nothing to do with our reality. When I let those thoughts take over, they took me to very dark places. Today I can identify that emotion, bringing it to the feet of the Lord as many times as necessary. I do not want to carry it alone. The Holy Spirit has been faithful, and each time He has led me down the path of deliverance, healing, and restoration. Thank You, Lord, for those spiritual conversations with You and Kristen.

I am sure that we all have emotional burdens to bring to the Lord. We should do it as soon as possible, because the longer we carry it alone, the heavier it becomes. Spiritual conversations in marriage include praying together and talking about spiritual truths. That is why it is so important not to be unequally yoked with unbelievers. Even as Christians we can have different interpretations of the Bible, but our foundation is the same. Together we build our home on the rock of Jesus Christ: "I am the way and the truth and the life. No one comes to the Father except through me" (John 14:6). If we agree on this absolute truth, we are at least starting on the same page.

We can evaluate how connected we are in spiritual communication by how comfortable we are praying together and sharing our spiritual journey. Do we feel free to pray and worship the Lord together? How much do we support each other in our spiritual struggles? Do we pray for each other? Do we read and share God's Word together? Do we share what we receive from God in our time alone with Him? Do we share what we learned in church on Sunday? Do we encourage each other to seek God in prayer and fasting? Sharing our spiritual journey without fear of judgement or pressure is a good indicator of healthy spiritual communication.

If we realize our spiritual communication is lacking, it is easy to become discouraged. This type of communication requires humility and spiritual discipline. It does not happen naturally, because our sin nature wants to isolate and hide. When we are vulnerable and open, Jesus shines His light on areas He desires to change. That is why we may feel uncomfortable sharing our spirituality with our spouse. If we begin to pray together and share what the Holy Spirit is speaking to us, we will begin to experience something supernatural, beyond what we could imagine. We can begin to walk on the water of our circumstances and experience firsthand that there is nothing impossible for God! Our job is to come to Him, hand in hand, with our eyes fixed on Jesus. He will perfect our faith. Springs of living water will flow from our hearts, and our communication will be divine.

CHAPTER 6
Conflict **Resolution**

So if you are presenting a sacrifice at the altar in the Temple and you suddenly remember that someone has something against you, leave your sacrifice there at the altar. Go and be reconciled to that person. Then come and offer your sacrifice to God.

Matthew 5:23–24 (NLT)

CONFLICTS ARE NOT THE PROBLEM; NOT RESOLVING them is. Conflicts in our relationships are inevitable, because we are imperfect humans who selfishly desire our own way. Marriage is no exception. No matter how compatible we are, we still have differences that create conflicts with our spouse. If we don't learn to resolve conflicts quickly, then they can become a crisis, leading us to sin against our spouse, breaking promises and hurting the one we vowed to love unconditionally.

In this chapter we will look at the most common types of conflicts and how to resolve them practically. Remember, God wants to bless our marriage. Learning to resolve conflicts is one way to walk in His blessing. God considers it a prerequisite to worship! (See Matthew 5:23–24.) Reconciliation is not only important for our relationship with our spouse but also for our relationship with God. He cares how we treat people and expects us to make things right with those around us. That doesn't mean it will be easy to do; it just means that He gives us the power to do it. Jesus said, "I have told you all this so that you may have peace in me. Here on earth you will have many trials and sorrows. But take heart, because I have overcome the world" (John 16:33 NLT). Marital conflicts definitely fit into the category of "trials and sorrows," but we can take heart because Jesus has given us the ability to walk in reconciliation. We are no longer slaves to sin and the flesh. Jesus has overcome the god of this world and given us the power to live in peace!

Over the years, Kristen and I have had several conflicts that spiraled into a crisis. Honestly, it is a miracle we are together today. And thankfully we are not just together but *happily* together. We eventually learned to resolve our conflicts before they become a crisis. The longer we leave the conflict unresolved, the bigger the problem becomes. If we take action and put into practice what God teaches us in His Word, then we can quickly restore peace again. In this book we are talking about a divine marriage, in which the presence of God is manifested. Where there is unity and peace, He is in our midst (Psalm 133). For that reason, the enemy persistently works against our unity, planting seeds of discord that later become a root of bitterness. Discord usually begins with different points of view. We allow the differences to become a conflict, which if not resolved becomes a full-blown crisis. It has a snowball effect, growing and gaining strength. If we do not stop it in time, it will crush everything in its path.

We are going to see how to stop this harmful cycle. First, though, we need to distinguish between differences, conflicts, and crises.

- **Differences** are perceptions of something from another point of view (such as the glass half full or half empty). Each person processes information differently and makes decisions accordingly. Having differences is not the same as having conflicts.

- **Conflicts** are differences that end in an argument each time they are mentioned (see Proverbs 17:14). We are not willing to agree to disagree. We don't respect each other's opinions, and we want to force our spouse to agree with our point of view.

- **Crises** are unresolved conflicts that are completely untouchable without escalating to a strong verbal and/or physical fight. The result is emotional and sometimes physical separation.

The devil's goal for us is separation and strife. God's goal is unity and peace. There is a constant struggle in our soul to decide what to do: will we allow ourselves to be carried away by our emotions, or will we submit them to our will? Remember, our emotions were made to follow our will, not our will to follow our emotions. So many couples navigate their relationship by emotions. "I feel that I love him." "I feel that I do not love her anymore." "I feel jealous." "I feel sad today." "I feel happy when ..." The list could go on. We can feel many things, but we must decide what is the truth. We must keep our emotions under control. If we let them control our life, then it becomes a roller coaster that nobody wants to ride.

When we realize our emotions are out of control, we need to stop, take a deep breath, and ask God for help to regain control. Then we need take responsibility and ask our spouse for forgiveness. There is no such thing as "You make me angry." We are all responsible for our own attitudes and actions. Having the humility to walk in forgiveness puts us on the road to restoration. Proverbs 17:9 says, "Love prospers when a fault is forgiven, but dwelling on it separates close friends" (NLT).

When we don't forgive, the price is costly. We hear from countless couples in crisis, on the edge of divorce, and they don't know how they got there. They are unaware at what point they "crossed the line of no return." I believe the "line" is when we intentionally stop walking in forgiveness. Somehow, we feel we have the luxury of not forgiving or asking for forgiveness. We live in denial of any negative consequences. We naively think we can keep making withdrawals of offense without making deposits of love and affection. But the day will come when our emotional bank accounts are empty. Kristen and I know too well how that works. We struggled, especially at the beginning of our marriage, with several untouchable issues. When we tried to work through them, the whole environment changed, and the conversation always ended in a stalemate. We would stop talking for several hours or take an indifferent attitude toward each other. I was especially guilty of this. I "pretended" to be offended sometimes for days.

Kristen would ask, "What's wrong?"

"Nothing," I answered.

"Are you still mad at me?"

"I'm not mad."

"Well, then you might want to tell that to your face!"

I look back and see myself as a sulking kid who refused to speak or let anyone touch him, but inside I was screaming for love and approval. Another time, Kristen and I started a conversation that quickly turned into an escalating conflict. I was about to default to one of my dramatic exits when I actually had a coherent thought (something that doesn't happen very often when we are fighting!): *Wait, this is ridiculous. I can't even remember what we are fighting about. At this point it's all melodrama.* So I came up with my best Mexican soap opera names and announced the end of the episode. (If you are not familiar with Mexican soap operas, I can't say I recommend them, but they have definitely mastered the art of melodrama. Kristen started watching them to learn Spanish. Then we both got hooked!) I think I chose the names María Kristina del Rincón and Luis Alfonso de Zaragoza. (Yes, my middle name really is Alfonso.) A few seconds of silence followed, and suddenly we started laughing. A little humor never hurts! The devil was trying to divide us, but we decided to call his bluff: "Enough! You are not going to make a spectacle out of us." We hugged quietly and then prayed for the Lord's help. We humbled ourselves before Him, asking forgiveness for letting our emotions get out of control, and took authority over every spirit of division, anger, strife, etc. The Word says, "Humble yourselves before God. Resist the devil, and he will flee from you" (James 4:7 NLT).

The enemy of our souls is a cunning script writer. He wants to make a tragic melodrama out of our lives. Kristen and I decided he will not write the script for our story. God has the last word! In those moments when tempers flare, it is better not to speak at all, since the enemy can use every word that comes out of our mouths against us. I don't know if it has happened to you, but when we want to resolve a conflict without the help of the Holy Spirit, it only gets worse. What we really want is to defend our point of view. We are emotional beings, and words and images affect us deeply. That's why movies are so successful—they move our emotions even though we know they are fiction. So it is with conflicts: they move our emotions even though most of what is said in the heated moment is not a true story.

To resolve a conflict, you need to want to resolve it. You need to decide, *Do I want to be right, or do I want a solution?* Many marriages are in crisis today because they are not willing to resolve their areas of conflict. A divine marriage is not a perfect marriage. It's a marriage that is willing to walk through the process of deliverance, healing, and restoration. As we have already discussed, God wants us to bless our spouse. Yes, we are different, but that is a blessing as Kristen explained in Chapter 3: Our Differences Are Our Strengths. We know we cannot avoid differences, but we can work on listening to one another before our emotions kick in. When we listen with the heart, we learn to love unconditionally. God is very wise, and that is why marriage is for life—He knew it would take us a lifetime to learn to love unconditionally.

The first step in resolving a conflict is to die to self. The goal is not for the other person to change so we can be happy. No, we *both* need to change. Several years ago, Kristen and I had a bad argument over something that wasn't even important. I stormed out of the room and left her talking to herself (something I never should have done). I went to my room fuming and said to God, "This is just who I am. It's how I am wired."

I heard the Lord say, "Then change."

"But it's my personality. How can I change that?"

"You can have the personality of Jesus through the power of the Holy Spirit."

"Father, how can I do that?"

"Ask Me for it with a sincere heart."

Right then I got on my knees and asked for help to become more like Him, "gentle and humble at heart" (Matthew 11:29). It has been a long process, and I am still in it. But looking back, I see real progress.

In Christ we can be more than conquerors. The Bible says we are more than conquerors, but there is a condition: are we willing to live in His love? (See Romans 8:37–39.) Are we willing to change through the power of the Holy Spirit and let His personality take control of ours? You may think this sounds unrealistic or overly spiritual, but remember: a divine marriage is supernatural. As God's children we have the opportunity to co-operate and collaborate with our heavenly Father.

Ideally, we want to take practical steps to resolve a problem before it escalates. There is a simple (but not easy) process for resolving conflicts that we have seen work well. Many times, conflicts are created by miscommunication or poor communication. If we make the effort to communicate correctly, we give ourselves an advantage to work successfully through conflicts. Healthy communication in marriage has two parts:

1. We express our thoughts or feelings in a way our spouse can understand.
2. We listen with patience and humility to receive feedback and understand our spouse.

This doesn't usually happen spontaneously. We have found most couples do best with a clear strategy. We recommend what is known as a courageous conversation.

How to Carry Out a Courageous Conversation

- Find the right time to talk. Plan a special time to discuss the situation. It is better to have it in private rather than in a restaurant or public place. If you have children, make sure they do not hear the conversation. Pick a time when you are not tired or stressed. Remove any distractions like television or social media.
- Check your motivation and attitude. Your intention should be to resolve the conflict, not win an argument.
- Pray before you start and ask God for help to listen with a sensitive heart.
- Decide before you begin that you are willing to change your point of view.
- Talk about only one topic at a time.
- Decide who will share first. Some find it helpful to write out their main points ahead of time so that they don't get focused on things that aren't important.
- Focus on the problem. Explain how you are affected by what your spouse is doing, not who they are as a person. Give information, not insults. Example: "I feel frustrated when you leave your clothes on the floor," not "I can't stand how lazy and messy you are."
- Avoid interrupting or defending yourself. Let the other person finish their thought, and when it is your turn, then you can share your perspective.
- Avoid exaggerating and don't use extreme words like "never" or "always."

[Handwritten note in margin: "This is good stuff. →"]

- Avoid accusing or judging your spouse's motivations. Example: "You always come home late because obviously I am not important to you." It's better to say, "I feel like I am not important to you when you come home late."
- Avoid using these words and phrases:
    - "separation"
    - "divorce"
    - "You always ..."
    - "You never ..."
    - "I can't stand this anymore."
    - "I can't put up with this."
    - "I hate you."
- Choose phrases such as:
    - "I feel like this when ..."
    - "It seems to me that ..."
    - "I would like to understand how ..."
    - "What I understand you are saying is that ..."
    - "I love you and I want to understand your heart. Forgive me if ..."
- Be careful how you share. Don't be sarcastic, raise your voice, or humiliate your spouse.
- If for some reason you aren't able to resolve the situation, then take a break, pray about it, and come back to it another time.

Courageous conversations carried out respectfully can be a great blessing because they open the door to healthy communication. Give it a try and remember you are on the same team. Your spouse is not your adversary. Your enemy is God's enemy, the devil, who wants to destroy your divine union since it represents the Kingdom of God here on earth.

For our struggle is not against flesh and blood, but against the rulers, against the authorities, against the powers of this dark world and against the spiritual forces of evil in the heavenly realms! (Ephesians 6:12).

Having conflicts in marriage is inevitable. But if we stay unified and continue to walk in love, we will win the battle the enemy is waging against our marriage. Together we stand on the promise that we are more than conquerors in God's love.

CHAPTER 7
Money **Matters**

The blessing of the Lord brings wealth,
without painful toil for it.
—Proverbs 10:22

MONEY MANAGEMENT IS ONE OF THE MOST IMPORTANT areas we need to address in our marriage. The problem is that we often don't give very much attention to it until we are in a financial crisis. This chapter is lengthy and detailed because I (Luis) want to save you the chaotic stress I created in our marriage before I learned God's plan for financial stability. I encourage you to study this together, because it can change your life as it has ours. We have personally put into practice everything I share here. Some of the information may not apply to your current situation, but keep it as a guide for the future. We will discuss the value of money and the importance of order in our finances. We will also cover the natural and spiritual laws God has provided in His Word to receive financial blessings and to bless others. Through both our personal experience and that of the many couples we have counseled, we are convinced that healthy finances are vital for a successful marriage. In fact, there are statistics that indicate money problems are one of the main causes of divorce.[13] The blessing and peace that come from having healthy finances can make the difference between living a divine marriage and becoming a divorce statistic. I encourage you to finish the entire chapter. You will see how simple and practical it is to follow God's wisdom. So find a comfortable place to read, grab a cup of coffee, and let's get down to business.

Money is meant to be a tool to supply our needs and to bless others. In other words, it is simply a means to an end. It should not be our focus. Unfortunately, money seems to take center stage in many marriages. Ask people if money is the center of their marriage, and most will say no. But let's look closer at how many couples live today. What are they most concerned about? Financial commitments. Where do they spend most of their time? At work, earning money. What topic do they talk about most? Purchases and expenses. What is one of the main reasons they argue? Debt and overspending. What keeps many couples together? Economic status and shared assets.

Money controls the environment in most households, but it should be the other way around—we should control money. God's Word warns us about the love of money:

---

13. Elizabeth Cole, "Money Ruining Marriages in America: A Ramsey Solutions Study," RamseySolutions.com, February 7, 2018, https://www.ramseysolutions.com/company/newsroom/releases/money-ruining-marriages-in-america.

For the love of money is the root of all kinds of evil. Some people, eager for money, have wandered from the faith and pierced themselves with many griefs (1 Timothy 6:10).

It doesn't really matter how much money you have; whether you're rich or poor, money can be your idol. If your life revolves around what you have or don't have, then you probably have a heart problem. Stop for a moment and be honest with yourself. Ask the Lord to reveal your heart. He explains how our attitude toward money reveals the condition of our hearts: "For where your treasure is, there your heart will be also" (Matthew 6:21). This means that the things we spend and invest our money in are what we value the most. In other words, our heart will follow our wallet!

Something I've learned is that we don't need to feel something to do it, but if we continually do it, then we will feel it. Let me explain. Suppose I have no interest in motorcycles, but a friend invites me to a race. I then start investing my money in motorcycle magazines, clubs, events, etc. Most likely, I will eventually buy a motorcycle. My desire to know more and invest more in motorcycles will grow. I will start prioritizing this new hobby as my interests change. Why? Because I decided to invest my money there, and what I invest my money in is what I begin to love.

That is why we must be very wise about where we spend our money. If we are not, then we can fall into the infamous "rat race"—spending our entire lives chasing the dream of financial stability but never achieving it. Working hard is not enough; we also need to work *smart*. It takes wisdom to make good financial decisions. Many people work hard to build a legacy. Some achieve it, but at what price? Failing health, neglected children, a broken marriage? Others never achieve their financial dream. They are always running after the proverbial carrot that is just beyond their reach.

God Is a God of Order

Living in disorder keeps us from the abundance Jesus promises in John 10:10. In my opinion, the abundance He refers to is peace. Nothing is more important than peace in our marriage. To achieve that, we must take control of the areas causing stress. God does not bless disorder. If we are self-controlled with money, we can enjoy the prosperity God promises. My definition of financial prosperity is having enough to cover our family's needs and to help others.

God calls His children to represent His Kingdom here on earth. Remember, according to Romans 14:17 His Kingdom is righteousness, peace, and joy. Financial stability is a Kingdom principle. It is an important element in establishing peace in the home. God has no problem with money. We are the ones who have the problem when we make it an idol. As I mentioned earlier, money is simply a tool. It can be used for good or for evil, depending on who is using it.

After much chaos, stress, humiliation, and prayer, I realized that I did not have control over money. It had control over me. Our marriage and family suffered tremendously. We lost our business, our house, our cars, our friendships, and above all our peace. I remember standing before the Lord's presence in prayer and asking, "What is happening, God? I love You, and everything I do I do for You." (That's what I thought at the time). "I am a family man, faithful to my wife. I have no vices. I serve in the church. What's more, I am even a leader! I consider myself a hardworking man who tithes and gives continuously. I don't understand why. Why am I in this terrible financial mess?"

As if it were yesterday, I remember hearing the Holy Spirit speak: "Yes, you have a financial mess, and I cannot bless disorder. I have created natural and spiritual laws for you to have financial peace. You have broken them and are suffering the consequences. If you are willing to walk the process, I can teach you how you can live a life of blessing." Of course, my answer was, "Yes, I am willing!" When you hit rock bottom, it's easier to cooperate!

Kristen and I started a new plan of action. We learned to use the natural and spiritual laws (principles) that exist within the Kingdom of God. (We will discuss these laws later.) ==We can't expect God to prosper us when we do not follow His financial principles==. It took us several years to put our finances in order and experience financial stability. Perhaps like me, you didn't receive education regarding money when you were growing up. It is like sex education at home—no one wants to talk about it, and they assume everyone already knows. Everyone thinks they know about money because they use it constantly, but not many people talk about it. Even in schools little is said about it. The lack of financial education has led to many conflicts in marriages.

Our prayer is that you and your spouse enjoy the blessing of financial freedom. I am not talking about the concept of having so much money that you can buy whatever you want. What I mean by financial freedom is living free from the bondage of debt. Debt is deceptive. It seems manageable in the beginning, but it eventually becomes a heavy burden, robbing you of peace, joy, and a good night's sleep! Let's look at the example of Raúl and Claudia (not their real names) who married a couple of years ago. They vowed lifelong love, in sickness and in health, for richer or for poorer, etc. Now they have two jobs, a baby, and only one car, which is causing stress in the relationship. They realize they are not in a position to buy a new car, but they go to the car dealership anyway "just to look." An hour later they drive away in a brand-new car. What happened? They fell into the trap of "Buy it now, pay it later." They were enchanted by the shiny chrome, the smell of new leather, the perfect color for Claudia, and all the newest tech for Raúl. Everything seemed perfect, even the kiss they shared as they signed their names. Wow, a new car! They never dreamed they could buy a new car.

Six months later, they started falling behind in their payments. They both picked up some extra hours at work, which meant leaving the baby longer in daycare. At that point, they were paying more for childcare and enjoying less time together. The pressure of having to work more hours added stress on their marriage. They were exhausted, impatient, and arguing more than ever before. By the time they came to talk to me, they were thinking of getting a third job! More money is not always the answer; staying in peace is. Buying a new car is great if you have an organized budget and know you can afford it. The problem is, very few people know if they can afford something or not. All it takes is a good salesperson and a "too good to be true" offer to lead us to a bad financial decision. External pressures affect internal peace. The questions Raúl and Claudia needed to talk about before they headed to the dealership were:

- How much can we afford?
- Will it bring stress?
- Is it the right time?

Before making a major purchase, you need an up-to-date budget to see if the price is within the percentage you can afford. Consider whether this decision is going to bring stress or a solution to the actual problem. Also, consider if it is the right time. Finally, if you are unsure, it is important to ask people who have financial stability for advice. On many occasions we ignore these steps and bring unnecessary external pressure into our marriage. I encourage you to consider these steps before going to the car dealership "just to look"!

Now let's talk about the financial laws I previously mentioned. We will start with the natural laws. These are basic principles that most people know but few people follow.

Natural Financial Laws

- Work
- Budget
- Save
- Invest

Work

Stable finances begin with being responsible and disciplined with our work and/or business. Working with integrity is number one on the list of natural financial laws. This point is extremely important. Being diligent and honest assures us that we are representing the Kingdom of God correctly. It is good to think about how to be better employees or entrepreneurs, as well as how to help the company, people, and clients who work with us. We should consider how we are doing with simple details such as getting to work on time, finishing what we start, being responsible with the resources entrusted to us, etc. It is good to have conversations as a couple about the jobs and/or or businesses we have. Keeping ourselves accountable takes humility. Transparency is never easy, but it saves us from conflicts down the road. Here are some things to consider for conversation:

- Are we being responsible with our time spent at work?
- Are we working ethically and honestly?
- Are we a good example for the people we work with?
- Do we keep the Lord Jesus present in our work and business decisions?
- Are we managing well the money we receive as compensation for our work?

When discussing our jobs, we should be supportive and careful not to be critical or judgmental. These types of questions are meant to help us self-reflect, not to bombard our spouse with uncomfortable questions! The idea is to stay accountable. Many couples consider their work totally independent of their marital relationship. I think this is a mistake, since in many cases it is where you invest the most time. Give your spouse a chance to talk with you about these areas. Listen to their input and pray about it. Remember that two are better than one.

In Proverbs 11, God talks about the importance of integrity:

> The LORD detests dishonest scales, but accurate weights find favor with him ... The integrity of the upright guides them, but the unfaithful are destroyed by their duplicity (vv. 1, 3).

Integrity is a powerful spiritual law. "So in everything, do to others what you would have them do to you" (Matthew 7:12 NLT). Many know this as the Golden Rule and don't realize that it is a biblical principle. If we are not careful about our integrity, then we will suffer loss. Dishonesty allows the enemy legal entry to rob us financially. Meditate on this. Close any doors that are open due to a lack of integrity.

Budget

The budget is the backbone of healthy finances. If we don't have one, then it will be difficult to achieve financial stability. Making a budget isn't hard—sticking to it is! It all starts with making a list of expenses. Interestingly, a 2019 survey revealed that 65 percent of Americans do not have a budget.[14] For years Kristen and I didn't have one. We tried several times, but the closest we could come was keeping a record of what we had spent. My thinking was, *If I don't have enough money, why make a budget? I'll just get frustrated. And if I have enough, why do it if I can buy what I want?* Kristen constantly asked me when we were buying something, "Does this fit in our budget?" My answer was, "If you need it, buy it, and God will provide." This was a serious point of conflict in our marriage until we both submitted it to God. We resisted the devil, and he fled from us (James 5:7). We tackled the problem both in the spirit and in the natural. We made a budget, and although it took a while, we finally were able to stick to it. This has brought peace to our marriage. The constant power struggle of my way or Kristen's way is over, because our budget makes the decision.

If we don't have a budget, then we are like a boat without an anchor. Any tide or current can shipwreck us. One of the

---

[14]. Mint, "Survey: 65% of Americans Have No Idea How Much They Spent Last Month," MintLife Blog, December 11, 2020, https://mint.intuit.com/blog/budgeting/spending-knowledge-survey/.

questions Kristen and I are constantly asked is how to make a budget. It is a simple, straightforward process. We complicate it by not having self-discipline. Before making a budget,

- prepare yourself mentally and pray,
- set aside a specific time,
- organize your expenses, and
- include your spouse.

Now you are ready to start by making a list of expenses. On a computer spreadsheet or in a notebook, begin to record any expenses that are made during the month. It's a good idea for both spouses to participate in this so that you do not forget any expenses. To help with this step, we suggest keeping your receipts (old school method) or using an expense tracker on your phone (digital method). Remember, this is not a budget; it is simply a list of all the expenses incurred. Start with what you spend weekly and monthly, or you can look at what was spent the previous year as an estimate. Be specific, honest, and thorough; don't leave anything out. If you do it right and take your time, then you will probably be 80 percent done. You can calculate the other 20 percent throughout the month as you review your list to check for forgotten items. The expense list is to record what you spend every day. The motivation for why it is spent is another topic that we will touch on later. Here is a very important reminder: making this list is *not* the time to fight with your spouse over their spending habits. Kristen and I know all about that. Do everything you can to avoid arguing, and just get it done!

Now write down your income, which is all the money that comes into your home. Write down everything, even small amounts. Things can get a little sticky here because some couples don't share how much they make with each other. I've heard men say, "I give my wife what she needs for the house. I can manage the rest." We encourage you to be transparent with each other. It's important not to skip any steps. If you follow them carefully, you will be amazed by the positive change in your relationship. Just keep in mind that it may get ugly before it gets pretty.

Divide your expenses by categories. Here is an example:

Categories
Donations
Housing & Utilities
Food
Transportation
Education
Health
Debt
Savings
Clothing
Recreation & Personal

This is only a guide; add any categories you feel necessary. If you are self-employed, then you will have to add a category for taxes (because they won't be taken out by an employer). Divide each category by your total income so that you get the percentage you are spending in each category. For example, if your income is $3,000 per month and you pay $1,000 a month for rent/mortgage, then divide $1,000 by $3,000. That equals 33 percent. This means you spend 33 percent of your income on housing.

Now that you have finished dividing all the categories by your income, compare them with the percentages on this table:

Categories	Examples	Suggested Percentages
Donations	Tithe	10%
	Offerings	5%
Housing	Mortgage/Rent, Home Insurance	30%–35%
	Utilities	5%–10%
Food	Groceries, Eating Out	7%–15%
Transportation	Car Payment, Gas, Insurance	10%–15%
Education	Uniforms, Books, Tuition	5%–10%
Health	Insurance, Prescriptions	5%–10%
Debts	Credit Card, Personal Loan	5%–10%
Savings	Emergency Fund, Investment	5%–10%
Clothing	Apparel, Footwear	2%–5%
Recreation & Personal	Entertainment, Hobbies, Gifts	5%–10%

These percentages are a guideline and can be adjusted as circumstances change. The sum of all your categories must equal 100 percent. This is known as zero-based budgeting. A budget that does not equal 100 percent is out of balance. For instance, if you are expecting a baby, there will be new expenses in health, household articles, and clothing. For those months whatever is added to those categories needs to be subtracted from another. We suggest that the percentage for housing does not exceed 35 percent, transportation 15 percent, and food 15 percent, because these categories are a priority for most people and serve as an anchor for the rest. When adjusting the others, try to focus on eliminating the debt category. Don't get used to having debt. It is better to live in freedom. The Lord tells us that His yoke is light, but debts are not. They are a heavy burden.

The goal in zero-based budgeting is that all income has a destination and falls within a designated category. When everything is balanced, all income must have a destination with zero income undesignated. Once we have the budget, the challenge is to maintain it. Kristen and I dedicate several hours every month to organize our household budget. I pick the first day of the month to set aside a few hours to schedule payments and prepare for any upcoming additional expenses.

Save

Saving is a learned discipline. Ideally, it is learned in childhood through the example of budget-savvy parents. If not, it will be learned the hard way through living the consequences of not saving! This was definitely my situation. Kristen and I lived in financial chaos for many years while I learned what she had already learned in her childhood. Saving is not easy, because it requires sacrifice—the sacrifice of saying no. I'll share a buying "rule" that has worked well for us: if either of us wants to buy something outside of our normal budget, we always wait and talk it through. Compulsive, on-the-spot buying is never an option. If we decide together to buy it, then the second step is to see where the money will come from. Can we spend less eating out this month? Will we need to use our savings? After evaluating these two steps, we decide if it can be done without throwing off our budget and robbing our peace. If it can't, then it is probably best to wait.

We can all learn to save if we allocate a percentage and a category for it in our budget. Having savings becomes a non-negotiable, like paying the rent. Think about it this way: if we had an emergency and needed $100 urgently, we would surely get the money from somewhere. It's the same thing with savings. If we set out to save a reasonable percentage of our monthly income and make it a priority, we will achieve it. For years, saving was not a priority for me. Kristen, on the other hand, is always saving something. Since the day we met, she has had a "secret stash" as she calls it. When we started our budget, we came into agreement for the first time about saving. We started with a small percentage, and we have experienced God's supernatural multiplication. I want to encourage you to start saving today, because tomorrow it gets easier. You can begin with a small savings account and put the agreed percentage of money there each month. The amount in the beginning may be minimal, but it is a step toward good stewardship.

You can have different savings accounts in the bank, or if you prefer to have access to your savings at home, you can have several savings envelopes with designated purposes.

Emergency Savings

We recommend saving at least $500 to $1,000 dollars (or the equivalent of two weeks salary) for situations that arise that are not in the budget. Examples include buying a new tire, getting the fridge repaired, paying an unexpected medical bill, etc. Remember, this savings is for emergencies, not patio furniture or a new watch!

1-3 Months of Income Savings

Once we have the emergency savings, now the focus is to save a month of income. This gives you peace of mind. If for some reason you are not able to work, you can be sure the expenses of that month will be covered. It is best to have three months saved but at least start with one. If you can save one, then you will be motivated to save more!

Specific Savings

These savings are for specific purposes, such as vacations, vehicles, and college funds. Dreams are great motivators. God wants us to live a life of peace, and saving helps bring that peace. Find your motivation and start saving today!

> Dishonest money dwindles away,
> but whoever gathers money little by little
> makes it grow (Proverbs 13:11).

Invest

When is a good time to start investing? When you have enough savings that some of it can be put to work for you. That means you will not need it to be immediately available. There are different types of investments that are managed in different ways. This is not a finance book, but it's important to have a general understanding of investment when talking about money management. Later, you can consult with an investment professional if necessary.

Types of Investments

1. Money market accounts: This type of savings account has a higher interest return than a bank savings account. However, they typically have a monthly charge for account management or for an insufficient balance. Make sure you investigate how much the minimum balance is to maintain the account without fees. If you don't have enough to avoid the fees, it would be better to leave the money in a bank (with less interest) but with the advantage of having all the money readily available.

2. IRAs, bonds, certificates of deposit (CDs): These are investment options that generate compound interest. However, it's important to note that most require the money to be out of reach for longer periods of time than the previous option. A general rule in low-risk investments is the longer the money is unavailable for your use, the higher the interest rate.

3. Stock market shares: In layman's terms, this means buying shares of public companies on the stock exchange. This can be done through a professional broker or on your own through an online brokerage. It is a good investment option; however, the risk is significantly higher than the previous options. A general rule is the higher the risk, the higher the gain. Of course, that means the risk of loss is higher as well.

4. Real estate: This is one of the oldest forms of investment. It has been tried and true for centuries. It means buying properties as assets, rentals, or resells. It's a great option; however, it usually requires a large investment.

5. Business opportunities: There is a big difference between a good idea and a viable business plan. Business opportunities can either be a thriving source of income or the biggest money and energy drain you could ever imagine. A good business involves planning, order, and clear budgets. Seek advice from successful businesspeople, and do not let yourself be pressured into a decision. Let your peace guide you and always include your spouse in the decision-making process. It's always better to have the money saved than to invest in a money pit.

Important note: lending money and charging interest to a brother in Christ or relative is not investing. Remember that when you loan money and charge interest, the person becomes a slave to you as the creditor.

> Just as the rich rule the poor,
> so the borrower is servant to the lender
> (Proverbs 22:7 NLT).

Do not charge a fellow Israelite interest, whether on money or food or anything else that may earn interest. You may charge a foreigner interest, but not a fellow Israelite, so that the LORD your God may bless you in everything you put your hand to in the land you are entering to possess (Deuteronomy 23:19-21).

When this passage from Deuteronomy mentions a "fellow Israelite," it is referring to the family of God. If you are Christian, then other believers are your brothers and sisters in Christ. This verse is very clear that we should not charge interest to a family member or fellow Christian who borrows from us. I personally feel it is better not to lend money at all. If someone is in need and I am able to help, I prefer to give it as an offering than to have a relationship strained over money owed.

All the investment opportunities mentioned above can be good options if you consider the benefits and risks. It's important to note that they all begin with saving. Remember, it is what you spend, not what you earn, that creates financial stability. In other words, if we spend everything we make, we will never produce wealth. We will live paycheck to paycheck our entire lives, most likely to become a financial burden for our adult children and never experience the blessing of money working for us when we invest it wisely.

Spiritual Laws

Now let's look at the spiritual laws pertaining to finances. This is one of the topics closest to my heart, as I have learned how life-changing it is to apply God's financial principles to our lives. God is never wrong, and when He gives us instructions, they are always for our good.

This is not a subject many couples talk about. For some people it can be uncomfortable because it is about giving. We know the saying, "It's better to give than to receive," but we don't normally live like this. For example, a child always has a harder time sharing a toy than receiving one. Our human nature is selfish. But sooner or later we are going to run into the issue of giving to others. Generosity is based on gratitude, compassion, and joy. It is linked to the heart. As I mentioned previously, God's Word says that where our treasure is, there our heart is too. I can't stop thinking about how much wisdom there is in Jesus' words. How we handle money will reflect the state of our hearts. I am sure we have all struggled in our hearts with the issue of giving.

God in His wisdom left us a clear map of how we can control our hearts with the simple act of giving. It is very important to talk about this issue and understand what your spouse thinks about generosity. You might find out that you think differently. But God wants us to be one in everything—body, soul, and spirit. We need to walk the process of maturity to experience the fruit of this unity. Coming to agreement in the way we approach spending and giving takes time.

As we saw in the natural laws, if we work with integrity, budget, save, and invest, we will prosper. Prospering doesn't necessarily mean we will be rich, (although some have that calling from God—see Deuteronomy 8:18), but we will live

Do you think differently than me?

an orderly life with enough to cover our needs and help others. Now imagine that there are laws that would multiply our resources exponentially. Wouldn't that be great? It would give us the freedom to do many things we dream about. Well, these laws exist, but few people know about them or how to implement them. This is not because they are secret, but because they must be spiritually discerned. They are spiritual laws most Christians ignore for lack of understanding and knowledge. They are in God's Word because He intends for us to use them with the guidance of the Holy Spirit. We need our hearts to be aligned with Him and have the correct motivations to see the fruit of these spiritual principles.

The Kingdom of heaven works differently than things here on earth. In the Lord's Prayer, Jesus says, "Your kingdom come, your will be done, on earth as it is in heaven" (Matthew 6:10). This means that heavenly laws can surpass the natural laws of earth. Remember, generosity is the key to abundance. Giving is a very powerful spiritual law. God says in His Word, "Give, and it will be given to you." It's that simple. Not only will you receive back what you gave, but even more! "A good measure, pressed down, shaken together and running over, will be poured into your lap" (Luke 6:38). If you apply this law in your marriage, then you will see the hand of God move financially in your favor.

The spiritual law of giving can be divided into two categories: tithes and offerings. Remember, spiritual laws work in the supernatural. They are not arbitrary or exclusive, and they work the same for everyone. As I mentioned earlier, Kristen and I come from very different financial backgrounds. We both needed to submit our ideas to the Word of God to receive the revelation of His Kingdom principles for our finances.

Let's Start with the Tithe

If you have been to church, you are most likely familiar with the term tithe. But what is tithing? Why give it? Who benefits from the tithe? Let's answer the first question. Tithing is a divine provision given to honor the Lord and protect our property. God says the tithe belongs to Him: "One-tenth of the produce of the earth, whether grain from the fields or fruit from the trees, belongs to the LORD and must be set apart to him as holy" (Leviticus 27:30 NLT). In biblical times, people's income came from the land and what it produced: "Honor the LORD with your wealth, with the firstfruits of all your crops" (Proverbs 3:9) The same principle applies to our income today. We honor Him, setting aside one-tenth (10 percent) of our income each month as holy to the Lord. We do that by giving our tithe to His church.

When we tithe, we are saying, "Lord, I honor You with my wealth. Everything I have comes from You. I trust You and transfer my money from the kingdom of this world to Your heavenly Kingdom." It is a divine transaction. God does not bless our money if we do not transfer it to His Kingdom; it is a law. Imagine it like changing your bank account. In an earthly bank account, your money is under the regulations of banks and financial systems. But when we transfer our money to His heavenly account, the guidelines change. This may sound like a fantasy, but stay with me. God asks you to transfer 10 percent of your income to His heavenly account, which is represented by the Church, the body of Christ. The word church (*ekklesia* in Greek) means 'government,' or in this case 'spiritual government.' It is a holy responsibility to be stewards of God's bank account! Sadly, some churches have been poor stewards, abusing their authority and manipulating in this area. But human failure does not change the principles God established. His blessing on our lives for being faithful with His tithe remains. You have to trust God and find a healthy church that handles its finances with transparency and wisdom. When we honor God in this, He protects our finances.

> "Bring the whole tithe into the storehouse, that there may be food in my house. Test me in this," says the Lord Almighty, "and see if I will not throw open the floodgates of heaven and pour out so much blessing that there will not be room enough to store it. I will prevent pests from devouring your crops, and the vines in your fields will not drop their fruit before it is ripe," says the Lord Almighty. "Then all the nations will call you blessed, for yours will be a delightful land," says the Lord Almighty (Malachi 3:10–12).

That's an amazing promise! But some people may say, "I've done that, but I haven't seen a change in my finances." Or "I started tithing, and things got better but then worse again." I think we can find answers by asking ourselves some questions. Remember the natural financial laws? Do we work with integrity? Do we have a budget we diligently follow? God says, "Give Me 10 percent, and I will bless the other 90 percent." Sounds like a good proposition, but let's take a deeper look. He's saying, "Give Me 10 percent." This is an exact number. He doesn't say, "Give me around 10 percent or whatever you want." He says 10 percent. How are we going to know what 10 percent is if we don't have a clear budget? Many couples do not know how much they earn or how much they spend. Let me answer another question that may be on your mind: why does it have to be so exact? I believe it is because God is just. Whether you have a lot or a little, the percentage is the same. The one who earns $1,000 a month has the same opportunity to give their 10 percent ($100) as the one who earns $10,000 a month ($1,000). The quantity will be different, but the heart test is the same for both.

Perhaps we do not have a clear budget, and we are not tithing correctly. This is not a legalistic concept. It's a matter of order, and God cannot bless disorder. It is also important to mention that our number one enemy, the devil, "prowls around like a roaring lion, looking for someone to devour" (1 Peter 5:8 NLT). He is trying to find a door to enter, and that door can be disorder, a lack of integrity in our business dealings, or a lack of faithfulness to God and His house.

Some couples may think, *We don't know how much we make, because we work in sales, and our income fluctuates.* The answer is easy; it just takes a little more time. Simply set apart 10 percent of each commission every time you are paid. If we have a mess in our finances, though, it is going to be difficult to be disciplined in this. For business owners without a fixed salary, it is best to set apart your tithe every time you take money out of the business for home or personal expenses. The reality is that if we have a budget and the heart to give, it will not be hard to do it correctly. The real problem is when we are looking for a way to give less or not give at all. At that point, it's not a money issue anymore—it's an integrity issue.

I have also heard, "Yes, we would like to give, but we cannot because we have debts." In this case the process is the same as for people without debts: trust God. Give first to God, and He will supply all your needs. It is a big step of faith to do this. God didn't say it would be easy; He tests our heart every time we receive money. God's ways are not always easy, but they are simple. We are the ones who complicate the concept of tithing.

And then there is this argument: "Tithing is not for today. The Jews were under the Law, but we live under grace." It is true that we live under grace, but tithing has nothing to do with the Mosaic Law. Tithing existed before it was mentioned in the Law of Moses. Abram gave 10 percent to the priest Melchizedek:

Melchizedek blessed Abram with the this blessing:

"Blessed be Abram by God Most High,
Creator of heaven and earth.
And blessed be God Most High,
who has defeated your enemies for you."
Then Abram gave Melchizedek a tenth of all the goods that he had recovered (Genesis 14:18–20).

As we see in this passage, Abram gave him 10 percent as an act of gratitude, not out of obligation. This is how our giving should be. There is a very special blessing when we give our first fruits to God. Melchizedek blessed Abram. There is always an action behind a blessing. We also see that Jesus comments on the importance of tithing and the condition of our hearts in Matthew 23:23.

Now let's answer the second question: who benefits from the tithe? Although we may think the beneficiary of the tithe is the church (and the pastors), the one who really benefits from the tithe is the one who gives it. Of course, there is a mutual benefit for church members and pastors. When members tithe, they have the benefit of enjoying all the church provides. But there is also a financial benefit for the giver as well. Tithing is a spiritual law that promises supernatural protection. Let's read Malachi 3:10–11 again:

"Your crops will be abundant, for I will guard them from insects and disease. Your grapes will not fall from the vine before they are ripe," says the LORD of Heaven's Armies. "Then all nations will call you blessed, for your land will be such a delight," says the LORD of Heaven's Armies (NLT).

Imagine you own a piece of land that represents your assets. When you tithe with the right heart, it is like putting a fence around that land so that the enemy cannot rob you. God says He will protect us. Tithing is a divine provision from God that protects us from the devourer.

Let's Look at Offerings

Offerings are the seeds that are sown within our land. Once we have fenced the land with the tithe, we are ready to sow (invest) in God's Kingdom and see the harvest grow. Our crops will be protected by natural financial laws and the tithe. Offerings are divided into three categories of giving: compassion, generosity, and investment.

Compassion Giving

This is when we give to people and organizations in need. For example, there is a person on the street who has nothing to eat or a brother at church who is going through a difficult situation and can't pay his rent. You give out of compassion, helping financially without expecting to receive anything in return. Or it could be a struggling ministry you feel led to help through a difficult time. It is about helping the poor or those in need. Our God is a compassionate giver, and that's why the Bible is full of instructions on giving: "Give to anyone who asks; and when things are taken away from you, don't try to get them back" (Luke 6:30 NLT).

God also tells us that if we give out of compassion, there is a reward:

> If you help the poor, you are lending to the LORD— and he will repay you! (Proverbs 19:17 NLT).

This is a promise. Although we give without expecting any compensation, God is faithful to His Word and will reward us in some unexpected way. Both individually and as a married couple, we must always be sensitive to the needs of others, as this shows a compassionate heart.

Generosity Giving

These offerings come from a generous heart, not in response to a specific need but simply because you are grateful for what you have and want to bless others. For example, if someone is waiting for their ride home, you say "No worries, I'll take you!" Or a friend mentions how much she loves your blouse, so you buy her the same one. Generous people see an opportunity to give and are the first ones in line. Generosity is a great quality, but it is important not to be rash in our giving. We need to be wise and sensitive to the Holy Spirit. Otherwise, we can give what we do not have or what does not belong to us. For example, you decide to pay for everyone's meal at a friend's birthday dinner, but the only money you have is for the rent that is due next week. You justify it with, "I'll give it now, and then I'll figure it out. God will provide." This is a mistake. We should give from what we have in the budget designated for giving. (We will see an exception to this in Investment Giving.) Or allocate it from a different area in which you know you can do without.

Otherwise, even if we have good intentions, we can give out of God's order. "Whatever you give is acceptable if you give it eagerly. And give according to what you have, not what you don't have" (2 Corinthians 8:12 NLT).
An important quality of this type of offering is joy.

> Remember this: Whoever sows sparingly will also reap sparingly, and whoever sows generously will also reap generously. Each of you should give what you have decided in your heart to give, not reluctantly or under compulsion, for God loves a cheerful giver (2 Corinthians 9:6–7).

God rewards the generous—not because they are seeking it but simply because that is His character. When we are generous, He entrusts us with more. It is a privilege to collaborate with God, blessing others in His name!

> Give generously to them and do so without a grudging heart; then because of this the LORD your God will bless you in all your work and in everything you put your hand to (Deuteronomy 15:10).

> A generous person will prosper; whoever refreshes others will be refreshed (Proverbs 11:25).

> You will be enriched in every way so that you can be generous on every occasion, and through us your generosity will result in thanksgiving to God (2 Corinthians 9:11).

Investment Giving

It is not very common to hear about this type of offering. The idea of an investment implies receiving a profit or return. Normally, we talk about helping others without expecting anything in return, so an investment offering sounds like a contradiction in terms. But it is in the Word of God. We make these offerings when we partner with God in His "business," with the projects God is doing through people and organizations. God is in the people business. He loves people, and He wants us to know Him and spend eternity with Him. For that to happen people need to hear about Him through the good news of the gospel of Jesus Christ:

> But how can they call on him to save them unless they believe in him? And how can they believe in him if they have never heard about him? And how can they hear about him unless someone tells them? And how will anyone go and tell them without being sent? That is why the Scriptures say, "How beautiful are the feet of messengers who bring good news!" (Romans 10:14–17 NLT).

God is looking to entrust His Kingdom to those who love and believe in Him. When we have His heart for the lost, He invites us to participate in His mission to rescue, free, heal, and restore lives. We call it the Great Commission. Jesus instructs us in Matthew 28:19–20:

> Therefore go and make disciples of all nations, baptizing them in the name of the Father and of the Son and of the Holy Spirit, and teaching them to obey

everything I have commanded you. And surely I am with you always, to the very end of the age.

We can reach beyond our personal sphere of influence by investing money in those who are living the Great Commission. The good news of Jesus is sent to the ends of the earth with money. Without it, missionaries can't be sent, water wells can't be built, starving children can't be fed, healing crusades can't rent tents, radio and television can't broadcast hope, abortion counselors can't reach desperate mothers, recovery centers can't care for addicts, shelters can't house the homeless, sex traffickers can't be apprehended ... None of these missions can continue without financial investment. When you invest in God's business, His mission, something wonderful happens. People hear the good news of Jesus, and their lives are transformed for eternity. The bonus is that you are blessed too!

Where and how much should I invest?

This type of giving is usually a larger financial commitment than simple generosity giving. It is important to ask God for a specific amount and give strategically. This is when it gets really exciting. We can give beyond our financial ability and still do it wisely when we believe God to provide before we give. For example, if God tells you an amount to give, but you don't have it, then respond with wisdom and faith: "Yes, Lord. When You give this amount to me, I will give it to Your Kingdom." God can surprise you with a special bonus or extra business. We know of one couple who received an unexpected insurance claim check from an accident 2 years prior! In our experience, when we have given large sums outside our budget, we usually give a small amount that we do have and wait for the provision for the rest.

It's important to wait on the Lord actively, taking a step of faith and putting your faith in action. I recommend that whenever you make an investment, you talk about it as a couple and pray for agreement and God's peace. Kristen and I are always amazed how God confirms the same amount to us that we should give. We like to write the amount on little pieces of paper and then give each other our paper. Just for fun, we count to three and look at the papers at the same time. It's exciting to know we are hearing God's voice! On a couple occasions our numbers have been different. We go back and pray, and if they are still different, then we go with the higher number. An offering should be given willingly with joy, not under pressure or manipulation or by acquiring a debt.

Every investment has a return. What is the return on investment in this case?

1. Souls saved and lives transformed
2. Personal blessing

The blessing can come in many ways such as your business and work, unexpected gifts, trips, discounts, etc. God blesses us in different ways, and He will always "outgive" us!

> Give, and you will receive. Your gift will return to you in full—pressed down, shaken together to make room for more, running over, and poured into your lap. The amount you give will determine the amount you get back (Luke 6:38 NLT).

It is important to note that God takes our commitments seriously. Don't withhold an offering you promised to give.

> Will a mere mortal rob God? Yet you rob me. But you ask, "How are we robbing you?" In tithes and offerings. You are under a curse—your whole nation—because you are robbing me (Malachi 3:8-12).

It is important to understand is that unlike the tithe, offerings are voluntary. However, when we make a vow to God, it becomes a covenant with Him. It is better not to make promises than to make them and not keep them.

> When you make a vow to God, do not delay to fulfill it. He has no pleasure in fools; fulfill your vow. It is better not to make a vow than to make one and not fulfill it. Do not let your mouth lead you into sin (Ecclesiastes 5:4-6).

Here's an example of what that might look like. One day two friends plan to meet for lunch, assuming each will pay for his own meal. When they arrive at the restaurant, one of them says, "Let me buy you lunch. I'll pay." He makes a commitment of his own free will; no one asked him to do it. But when the bill comes, he changes his mind: "You know, I think it's better if we just pay for our own." What would happen? His friend would probably feel bad, like he was cheated. He didn't ask him to do it, but his friend committed himself and then didn't follow through. It is better not to say anything if you do not have the intention and motivation to do it. That is why Scripture says, "Just say a simple, 'Yes, I will,' or 'No, I won't.' Anything beyond this is from the evil one" (Matthew 5:37 NLT). If this has happened to you and you have committed to God to give an offering but have not yet done so, then make the effort and just do it. If you have overcommitted yourself and don't have the means to do it, then repent, ask God for forgiveness, and start over. "If we confess our sins, He is faithful and just to forgive us our sins and to cleanse us from all unrighteousness'" (1 John 1:9 NKJV). It is also a good idea to speak to the person or ministry with whom you made the commitment and let them know you have changed your plans.

I encourage you, together with your spouse, to invest in ministries and missionaries that bring souls into the Kingdom and alleviate suffering in the world. It's important to be well-informed and make the decision prayerfully. Our investments should have a good return, measured in lives that are transformed. Otherwise, it is a poor investment, and we are not being good stewards of what the Lord has entrusted to us.

Before we end this chapter, let's take some time for self-reflection:

1. We surrender our hearts to Jesus and allow Him to take control of our financial life and marriage.
2. We ask for forgiveness if we have violated the laws He has set in place to bless us. We can begin today to change our habits.
3. We are proactive about giving to God's vision and mission.

If your financial situation is not what it should be, don't be discouraged. It's never too late to put these laws into practice and experience God's grace. Jesus is coming soon, and He has commissioned us to prepare the way for His return. Money is needed for the gospel to advance, and God is looking for those who have healthy finances to partner with Him.

==Order is the key to prosperity, and generosity is the key to abundance.== ==Remember, change doesn't happen overnight; healthy finances take time to build.== The important thing is to be diligent. Perseverance is the foundation of success. We pray that what we shared in this chapter helps you put your home in financial order. May you experience the power of God as you partner with Him through your generosity!

> Now I commit you to God and to the word of his grace, which can build you up and give you an inheritance among all those who are sanctified. I have not coveted anyone's silver or gold or clothing. You yourselves know that these hands of mine have supplied my own needs and the needs of my companions. In everything I did, I showed you that by this kind of hard work we must help the weak, remembering the words the Lord Jesus himself said: "It is more blessed to give than to receive" (Acts 20:32–35).

CHAPTER 8
Parenting **Principles**

*He will turn the hearts of the parents to their children,
and the hearts of the children to their parents.*
— Malachi 4:6

IT'S INCREDIBLE TO THINK THAT OUR THREE LITTLE bambinos are all grown up and forging their own paths as adults. There is nothing more satisfying for parents than watching their children grow up to be responsible and happy adults, full of purpose and love for God. And there is nothing more painful than watching them struggle with addictions, depression, insecurities, rebellion, and a lack of vision. Every parent wishes the best for their children, but sometimes we don't know how to guide them. Being a parent is a complicated job, and when we leave the hospital with our little bundle of joy, no one offers us a user manual. But the good news is, God already gave us a manual for life. In the Bible we find treasures of wisdom to guide our children.

In this chapter we want to share with you what has worked for us personally and other families we know—not theories but practical advice that works in real life! Parenting is a very important role that affects the entire environment of our home. If there is no unity in the way we raise our children, there will be a lot of stress in the marriage and disorder in the home. Whatever decision you make regarding your children, do it together. It is very important that your children see you as one. It's amazing how clever kids are at identifying the weakest link to get what they want! If you decide to apply something from this chapter (and we hope you do), agree on it first as a couple. Then make a strategy and put it into practice together.

When it comes to parenting, the order of the factors does alter the product ($a + b + c = x$, but $c + b + a \neq x$). If we correct our children for misbehavior before giving them clear instructions, we will not achieve the same result as when we give them clear instructions and then correct them if they do not obey. The same happens if we give them too many freedoms before teaching them how to handle that freedom or if we put too many limits on them when they are mature enough to handle more of their own decisions. The key is to instruct our children in the right order, setting proper limits and freedoms at the right time.

Later we will discuss the different stages of development and discipline, but we need first to look at ourselves as parents. We should examine our hearts before God and see what our attitude is towards raising children. We know we love them, but maybe we don't really love the process of raising them! God has a great purpose for our children, and He is trusting us to be diligent in nurturing and guiding them. As the saying goes, "If you don't know where you're going, you've already arrived." Children must be purposefully guided in a specific direction.

> Children are a heritage from the LORD,
> offspring a reward from him.
> Like arrows in the hands of a warrior
> are children born in one's youth (Psalm 127:3–4).

For an arrow to hit the target, it must be skillfully aimed in the desired direction. We need to know what the target is for each child and consider their unique gifts and abilities. As we pray for God to reveal His plan for them, it's important to submit our own desires so that we don't attempt to live our frustrated dreams through them. Our children are God's children first, created for a divine purpose. Ultimately, they belong to Him. We have the incredible privilege of being responsible for them for a short time to direct their hearts, like arrows, back to their eternal Father. As parents, we should make the most of that time!

Another important foundation of child rearing is to make the marriage the center of the home. In Mexico there is a common question that young couples are often asked: "Tienes familia?" ("Do you have a family?") What they are really asking is, "Do you have children?" Having children should not be the same as having a family. When a couple marries, they form a family, and their union is the center of that new family. Children become *part* of the family unit, not the center. This means our decisions should not only take into consideration the needs of the children but also our needs as a couple. Children are only going to be in our care for a few years, but marriage is for life.

In Luke 2:52 we are told, "Jesus grew in wisdom and

stature, and in favor with God and man." Leading our children to be like Jesus is an incredible privilege and we need to be intentional in guiding their hearts. Children need lots of love, affection, and affirmation. They also need constructive discipline. Loving our children is the easy part. Giving consistent direction and discipline, though, is challenging. We found the following key principles to be life-changing during the different stages of raising our children.

Correction Stage (0-5 years approximately)
The target goal is to form self-control and obedience.

At this stage, it's okay to micromanage a child's day, giving limited options without much explanation. If they are presented with too many choices, young children tend to think the whole world revolves around them. When they are small and innocent, it seems insignificant when we let them always have their way by choosing the color of their cup, the clothes they wear, the food they eat, the activities they do, etc. When Mom tells her baby boy that he can't eat any more sweets and his little lip trembles and he starts crying, he looks adorable and makes her laugh. She may even take a video and get lots of likes on social media. But when he grows up and continues demanding to have everything his way, it will not be so cute. Nobody wants to see a video of a sixteen-year-old's temper tantrum, kicking and screaming for not getting the car he wanted! Obviously, life is not always how we want it to be. The best way to learn self-control is to not always receive everything we want when we want it.

We must set clear limits and expectations. The best way to be clear is when we look our children in the eye while talking to them and ask them to respond so we know they have understood the instructions. No shouting up the stairs hoping they will listen! We should make sure they know what we are expecting so we can give appropriate consequences. The key is to be consistent and keep our word. It is counterproductive to give directions and then not follow through with discipline if they do not obey.

> To discipline a child produces wisdom, but a mother is disgraced by an undisciplined child (Proverbs 29:15 NLT).

Some versions of the Bible mention the "rod of discipline," which may be an effective option depending on the child and the situation. Keep in mind that any type of discipline, including a verbal scolding, can be abusive. Remember, the consequences should never be severe or embarrassing and should not be applied when we are angry. It is so important to have our emotions under control before implementing any type of discipline. The purpose of the consequence is for the good of the child, so it should always be given with love and acceptance. Modeling self-control is a way of teaching them self-control. We cannot expect from them what we cannot do.

It is also very important to be clear about limits and expectations.

- "You can play here, but remember you cannot jump on the couches."
- "You can look at the ornaments in Grandma's house but not touch them."
- "You can run outside but not inside the church."
- "You can play in the garden, but don't pick the flowers."

The goal is first time obedience. Ideally, we want to train our children to obey the first time they receive an instruction, not after ten different threats. We must be diligent and consistent with the follow through. This part is difficult for parents since most of us are lax about keeping our word, and children realize that. When they learn not to take our authority seriously, it causes significant harm. Growing up without respect for authority affects them tremendously in their relationship with family, society, and God. Parents, we must be self-disciplined when we discipline. Our children's well-being depends on it.

Training Stage (6-10 years approximately)
The goal is to form values of respect and continue to reinforce obedience.

Now is the time to get used to explaining everything! If you already have children in this age, then you know very well that you can spend most of the day answering the infamous "Why?". In this stage we continue to reinforce everything from the previous stage, but now we help our children form values associated with the "why." Each answer is an opportunity to guide their hearts. Here are some examples:

- "You can play here but remember not to jump on the couches because they will get dirty and can break."
- "You can look at the ornaments in Grandma's house but don't touch them because she will be sad if they break."
- "You can run outside but not inside the church because we should respect the people talking there."

❧ "You can play in the garden, but don't pick the flowers because they are God's creation. He wants us to take care of everything He makes. And if you pick them, no one else can enjoy them."

In this stage we help our children see beyond their natural "me first" response. We teach them to have respect for themselves, people, authorities, nature, and, above all, God.

The ultimate goal of instruction and discipline is to win the hearts of our children with love. We do not want to frustrate them with expectations that are not clear. When they disobey, it must be because they chose to do so; then they are responsible for the consequences. In our house we did not "punish" our kids. We made sure they understood that any discipline was a consequence of their own decisions. We tried to be clear about what we expected and what the consequence would be if they didn't obey. And then they chose to obey or not obey. It was their responsibility.

When we were not clear on what we expected, it provoked stress and frustration in our children. One thing we used to help clarify expectations was a kitchen timer. Since they did not have a clear understanding of time, we did not want to frustrate them by asking for something they did not know how to do. I (Kristen) used to say, "Pick up your toys because we're leaving now." That caused frustration because sometimes they were in the middle of an activity that was important to them. So I tried giving them a time limit: "You have five minutes, and then you need to put everything away." I would return five minutes later, but they were still playing! I thought it was disobedience, but it was actually a lack of understanding about time. Yes, most six-year-olds can tell time, but that doesn't mean they have a sense of time. What was the solution? A kitchen timer. I said, "I'm going to set it for five minutes, and when it beeps, I want you to pick up your toys." It worked! Kids will be kids. Remember, not all lack of compliance is defiance.

When we teach respect, we need to show respect. Children learn more by watching our example than by listening to our words. It is an opportunity for us all to grow. We can show respect by listening to our children. When we walk into a room of bickering siblings and see a cracked tablet on the floor, the temptation is to discipline them immediately without hearing their explanation. In our family, the attitude behind the action and not the action itself is what determined the severity of the consequences. Sometimes children act foolishly simply because of immaturity and not rebellion. As parents, we need to discern the difference. Did they drop the tablet because they were distracted or because they were angry? Our goal should be to mold the hearts of our children, not their behavior. If we focus only on behavior, they will grow up frustrated, rebellious, and less capable of making good decisions on their own. But if we mold their hearts, then when they grow up, they will not only choose what is right, but they will also know why they are doing it.

Instruction Stage (11-15 years approximately)
The goal is to form personal virtues and good character.

Oh, blessed adolescence ... That might sound like an oxymoron, like a clash of two contrary words, but adolescence truly is a blessing. It is an incredible opportunity to build a bridge of virtue between childhood and adulthood, where we walk hand in hand toward their purpose in life. Here we have two key concepts: building and walking together.

If we did our job well in the first two stages, then our children already have a firm foundation of self-control, obedience, and respect. (And if they don't have it yet, don't lose heart. Keep working on it!) At this stage, we help them build good character and strong virtues on that foundation. Here, our children begin to embrace biblical virtues as their own. They are no longer just ideas from their parents or church. However, we can't expect them to develop these virtues alone. We have to keep walking with them. When we are confronted day in and day out by a rebellious teenager, the temptation is to let go of the reins and throw in the towel. But that is when they need us most. Maybe their mouth is yelling, "Go away! Leave me alone!" But their heart is yelling, "I feel lost in this confusing world. Don't leave me alone."

Parenting is not for the faint of heart. We need the strength of the Lord to accomplish the task of leading our teens to a life of blessing. The strategy for this is found in Deuteronomy 6:5–7:

> Love the LORD your God with all your heart and with all your soul and with all your strength. These commandments that I give you today are to be on your hearts. Impress them on your children. Talk about them when you sit at home and when you walk along the road, when you lie down and when you get up.

According to these verses, we set an example by our own relationship with God. We then practically live out that relationship, instructing our children by example as we walk with God together. It is not just sitting them down to have a Bible study. It's better for all of life to be a study of God and His goodness! As we know, life is not all sunshine and roses. Bad things happen, and they are an opportunity to teach our children about the wages of sin, our enemy, and spiritual warfare. The book of Proverbs is an extraordinary resource in this formative stage. We can use it to instruct them about their relationship with God, parents, friends, the opposite sex, and money.

It is important that our children see the benefits of following God and His commandments. It's not enough to say, "Because I say so," "That's what God says," "You'll regret it if you don't," or even worse, "God is going to punish you if you don't." To form values that will last their lifetime, young people need to understand the benefits rather than just the negative consequences.

As parents, we must choose our battles wisely. Decide as a couple which things are nonnegotiable and which are flexible. We can't say "No" to everything. Examine the motivation behind their actions. It is not wise to continually argue with your daughter or son about their messy bedroom, tattered jeans or less than perfect grades at school. Focus on their character and their heart toward God and people more than anything else, and be sure to give lots of encouragement. Remember, you are building a bridge that must be wide enough so they are not suffocated by religiosity and oppressive rules but that also has protective barriers high enough that they do not fall into the abyss of addictions and sin. Above all, let your children know they are not alone—you are with them all the way.

Relationship stage
(16 years and older approximately)
The goal is to affirm vision and purpose.

It is important to move to this stage gradually. Some young people are mature and responsible beyond their years, but most are not. Emotional and spiritual maturity, more than physical age, are what set the pace for moving into this stage. Many teens think by the time they turn 18, they are automatically adults, ready to face life alone. They think, "I'm 18 now. I can do what I want!" We want our children to be independent, but as long as they live at home, they need to show that they can make consistently good decisions. We can gradually give them more responsibility and independence, observing their heart attitudes in the process.

Our role begins to change from one of authority to friendship. The biggest mistake we've seen parents make is assuming the role of friendship too soon. Some parents allow their young children to relate to them as friends. Then when they grow up and get into serious trouble, these parents want to reverse the role and implement their authority. It should happen the other way around. Parents should be the authority over their children until they mature and can govern themselves. Then we can take on the role of mentor and friend.

Just like children, teens, and young adults need a great deal of affirmation. Life is hard, and there is a lot of pressure to achieve and "be somebody." They don't need more pressure at home. What they do need is a constant voice affirming that they are already somebody and that their value does not come from what they do. They need to know that achievement is good, but it does not determine their worth.

Their value comes from being a beloved son or daughter of the perfect, eternal Father. And their achievements develop from the purpose they find in their relationship with Him. As parents, we can be the most positive or the most destructive force in the lives of our children depending on whether they receive our affirmation and protection or our rejection and indifference. Even when they leave home and start their own families, it is important to give them support with words of encouragement and wisdom.

Luis and I have enjoyed all the stages with our children, but especially their adolescence and teenage years. Their teen years were pretty peaceful because we paid the price in the first two stages of their lives. When they were small kids, it was anything but peaceful. Correcting, disciplining, affirming and instructing was a 24/7 job. We still had to be aware and walk closely with them in their adolescence and teen years, but we knew they already had the values and discipline necessary to navigate life successfully. Of course, they weren't perfect by any means. Some of their life lessons were tough with painful consequences, but they had moldable hearts and grew from those experiences (thank God!). Today, they are awesome men who love God and are passionate about His Kingdom. For Luis and me, that is the parenting bullseye. Everything else—their ability to earn a living, start a family, help society, use their skills and talents, achieve their dreams—grows from there.

> Don't let anyone look down on you because you are young, but set an example for the believers in speech, in conduct, in love, in faith and in purity (1 Timothy 4:12).

We believe God's promises are trustworthy. We don't always see results as quickly as we want, but we can trust God to be faithful and honor His Word. Proverbs 22:6 says,

> Direct your children onto the right path,
> and when they are older, they will not leave it (NLT).

This promise is conditional—it's up to us to do our part. The command "direct" is for parents, not for church leaders or schoolteachers. In this verse, the Hebrew word to direct is *chanak*, which means 'to train, to discipline.' It is also used 'to dedicate.' This is the same word that was used in the Bible to dedicate the temple of God. *Chanak* is a multidimensional word, just like the role of being a parent. It refers to guiding children toward a specific goal with clear expectations (train), taking care that they stay within the established limits (discipline), and doing everything to honor God (dedicate). It is hard work, but the reward is great.

Remember, you need to be realistic. When young adult kids leave home and start making their own decisions, they don't always choose the "right" way. This can happen because of poor parenting or because of their own folly. Whatever the reason, it is important to emphasize that there is no condemnation in Christ Jesus. If that is your situation, please do not feel condemned or hopeless. What you could not achieve then in the natural, you can now do in the spirit. Repent of any failure as a parent and dedicate yourself to praying for your children, declaring that God's purposes will be fulfilled in their lives and that the enemy no longer has authority over them.

Each stage we go through as parents brings its own challenges and rewards. If you don't remember anything else from this chapter, remember this: **the best way to parent is a combination of clear expectations, consistent consequences, and lots of affection and affirmation**. It worked for us. Sometimes people make comments to us like, "Your kids turned out great." As if we just got lucky. But the truth is, they weren't always "good kids." Like all children, they each had their bad and sometimes *very* bad moments. Those moments motivated us to do something to help them. We took parenting classes and invested time, energy, and money in learning how to raise them better. There is a saying in Spanish: "Todo lo bueno cuesta." ("Anything good is costly.") When it comes to parenting, there is no price too high to pay to see our children walking happily in God's purposes. Be encouraged! All things are possible for those who believe.

Chapter 9

New Beginnings—
Blended Families

"For I know the plans I have for you," declares the Lord, "plans to prosper you and not to harm you, plans to give you hope and a future."
—Jeremiah 29:11

GOD IS THE GOD OF NEW OPPORTUNITIES. HIS Word says His mercies are new every morning (Lamentations 3:22-23). This means that every day we have the opportunity to receive God's grace to change the course of our lives. This chapter is for those who have experienced divorce or the death of a spouse and are now in a new marital relationship. If you have been through one of these painful experiences, we know it is not a comfortable subject, but it is important to address. For you to walk in all God has for you this new season, you need to make sure your heart is ready to receive it.

An unwanted divorce is one of the deepest emotional pains anyone can endure. It is an agonizing cocktail of betrayal, abandonment, rejection, grief, and loss. When we understand the power of being one, it gives us more insight into why divorce is so harmful. In Matthew 19:6, Jesus says, "So they are no longer two, but one flesh. Therefore what God has joined together, let no one separate." When we get married, we do not complete each other; rather, we complement each other. This means that we can be complete in God before marriage. But we cannot be complete after a divorce without divine restoration. Something supernatural happens when we make a marriage covenant before God. We become one. This is why divorce is so traumatic. When something is complete and then torn apart, it is no longer whole. What remains are two broken parts. It is a long and painful process to become whole again.

We must carefully rebuild with God those places of the heart that were damaged by the thief of divorce. This damage is often experienced in the areas of trust, security, acceptance, peace, joy, relationships with our children and friends, and our dreams for the future. They are ripped from our lives by the enemy who comes to kill, steal, and destroy. That's why God says in His Word that He hates divorce:

> "For I hate divorce!" says the LORD, the God of Israel. "To divorce your wife is to overwhelm her with cruelty," says the LORD of Heaven's Armies. "So guard your heart; do not be unfaithful to your wife" (Malachi 2:16 NLT).

This Scripture says the Lord hates divorce because it is overwhelmingly cruel. But there is hope for those who have gone down that long and painful road:

The Lord hears his people when they call to him for help. He rescues them from all their troubles. The Lord is close to the brokenhearted; he rescues those whose spirits are crushed (Psalm 34:17–18 NLT).

God understands the pain in this world. He is the God of hope who walks with us toward restoration. We fail, but God—say it out loud with me—God is the God of new opportunities!

In order to receive the new, we need to heal from the past. We cannot enter a new relationship and expect it to succeed without going through a careful restoration process. Regardless of whether you are just entering a new relationship or have been together for years, take time today to let God restore your heart. If you don't, then you will bring the old pain, guilt, regret, and bitterness into your present marriage. Repentance is key to leaving negative experiences behind.

Repent

The first step to being free and loving again is repentance. Even if the divorce was not your desire, breaking a covenant made before God is serious business. We are not talking about condemnation, which is diabolical and points us away from God. We are talking about repentance and conviction, which is taking responsibility before God for what we did wrong, asking for forgiveness, and leaving it nailed to the cross of Calvary. It no longer belongs to us, and it is important not to pick it up again.

Our God is a God of grace. We see a beautiful picture of His grace in the Bible in the parable of the prodigal son. Jesus tells the story of a son who leaves his father's house, squanders his inheritance on wild living, and ends up feeding pigs to survive. He then comes to his senses and returns home. Humbled and ashamed, the son repents and asks his father if he can work as a servant in his home.

> But the father said to his servants, "Quick! Bring the best robe and put it on him. Put a ring on his finger and sandals on his feet. Bring the fattened calf and kill it. Let's have a feast and celebrate. For this son of mine was dead and is alive again; he was lost and is found." So they began to celebrate (Luke 15:22–24).

==Grace is receiving what we do not deserve.== We experience God's grace when we leave our filthy attitudes and actions with the pigs as the prodigal son did and return to our Father's house.

We know couples who come from very difficult backgrounds and have experienced painful divorces. They repented and sincerely asked God, their ex-spouse, and their children for forgiveness for the terrible damage they caused. They returned to their heavenly Father's house and received His grace for a new beginning. They now live a new life in Christ without condemnation and are walking the process of restoration. When we sincerely repent for breaking our marriage vows, something supernatural happens, and God gives us a new opportunity. He offers peace and joy, replacing the guilt and shame.

Obviously, we are not promoting divorce. We do, however, promote the grace of God for those who repent and return to the Father's house and are walking the restoration process with everyone involved. The process is not easy, and it would be better to never have to go through it. God finds no pleasure in our suffering. He is a good Father, full of mercy and grace, who is waiting to celebrate our return home.

Forgive

The second step to being whole again is forgiveness. Many offenses are inflicted during a separation and divorce. You must be very intentional in the process of forgiving. Every time you remember a bitter situation with your ex-spouse, you need to forgive again. Don't try to forget or just ignore it. Forgive and turn the offense over to God. He is the One who brings justice for you. Forgiving is a way to remove yourself from the equation between God and the offender. When you forgive, you remove the obstacles for God to work on your behalf. When you do not forgive, it is like bringing past offenses into your present, and this will affect your new relationship. ==Forgiving is an act of the will; it is not a feeling.== It's about letting go. To receive the new, it is essential to let go of the past.

This step is also important for those who have experienced the death of a spouse. After the loss of a loved one, the tendency is to remember only the good. However, it is not healthy to have unresolved emotions. No human being is perfect, and many times mistakes have consequences that last even after we have left this world. It is important to forgive those failures to be completely free and receive the new.

Surrender

The third step is to surrender to Jesus. Surrender means to let go of everything. When we truly surrender to Jesus, we let go of the past with its sorrows, failures, and joys, as well as the present and the future with their hopes and fears. We cannot be whole and give ourselves completely to the new if we live in the memories of the past. It is important to give thanks for the good and forgive the bad without living in those moments. It is okay to revisit the moments, but we must not stay there. Give the memories to God and ask Him for help not to set up camp in that place. The same goes for thoughts of the future. Shake off the fear of the "what ifs" ("What if the same thing happens to me again?", "What if my children get even more hurt in the process?", etc.). Decide to trust again and maintain healthy expectations.

Remember, your new spouse is a unique person. Guard your heart from making comparisons. Surrender your fears to Jesus. Every marriage has moments of adjustment and challenge; these times do not mean pain and failure again. The enemy is an expert in fabricating negative scenarios in our minds, and we are experts in believing them! God paid a high price for our freedom, and we must walk in it, taking "captive every thought to make it obedient to Christ" (2 Corinthians 10:5).

Embrace

The fourth step is embracing the new with all its joys and challenges. We will now look at practical tips to embrace the new and help you build a successful blended family.

Blended Families

A blended family is one in which one or both spouses have children from a previous marriage. Statistics indicate that about 50 percent of today's families in the United States are blended families.[15] The family dynamic is not the same as with the first marriage. Every family has its own culture. When people marry, they bring together the family cultures in which they were raised. Blended families have the added dynamic of a previous marriage, adding the children and ex-spouse into the mix. It is important to be realistic and to prepare for a lengthy process of adapting in the first months and even years of your lives together. It takes a great deal of patience, communication, and intentionality to build a new family. In our years of giving marriage advice, we have found that some couples start their new family thinking they will be able to navigate the challenges without any preparation or special attention. This is naive and unrealistic. We believe the first step toward success in a blended family is to recognize your situation is different. You have unique challenges and need to be proactive in seeking the wisdom of God.

Here are some points to discuss in the process of adapting:

- ties to the past
- family culture
- healthy boundaries
- blended finances

---

15. "Stepfae Stepfamily Foundation Inc., accessed August 29, 2021, https://www.stepfamily.org/stepfamily-statistics.html.

Ties to the Past

When a new blended family is formed and all now live under the same roof, special attention must be given to the children. In many cases, they are expected to adapt automatically to their parent's new relationship, but it doesn't work like that. In the heart of every son or daughter is the need to be loved by their biological parents. Divorce and death leave a gaping hole in the heart. The idea of "Don't worry, they'll get over it" is neither fair nor realistic. Many adults today carry the scars of their parents' divorce. Remember, divorce is not God's plan; it is devastating and difficult for children to navigate. The feelings of abandonment and rejection are overwhelming, and the enemy is an expert at making children feel everything is their fault.

Physical, emotional, and spiritual ties to their parents are embedded in children's DNA. It is important not to expect them to "embrace the new" by leaving the past behind and forgetting about it. That is not going to happen, nor should it happen. The memories, both good and bad, will always be in their hearts. Attempts to rush their healing with comments like "This is our reality now, so we have to be realistic and move on" produce resentment against their mom or dad and the new spouse who is now part of their lives. It's better to gently include them in the new relationship without devaluing the importance of their relationship with their biological parents. Don't minimize their emotional pain; emotional and physical loss is traumatic. Walking your children through their pain is part of the process. Being patient and present are the keys to healing and accessing their hearts. It is important to encourage the children to strengthen their relationship with the parent who isn't present. (They do not need the burden of your negative feelings towards your ex-spouse.) This isn't always possible, as in the cases of an absent parent or an unwilling child, but the important thing is to make sure you are part of the solution and not making a hard situation worse. It takes wisdom to navigate these uncharted waters. The Bible tells us, "If you need wisdom, ask our generous God, and he will give it to you. He will not rebuke you for asking" (James 1:5 NLT).

The challenge is not only with the children. Spouses may be dealing with moments of doubt, unwanted comparisons, and overreactions to anything that reminds them of the past. The divorce rate in blended families is greater than in first marriages. Be extra diligent in caring for your new family, but do not live in worry or fear. Fear of failure robs your joy and undermines the success of your marriage. It is so important to hold on to God's Word. Second Timothy 1:7 says, "For God has not given us a spirit of fear and timidity, but of power, love, and self-discipline" (NLT). With the help of the Holy Spirit, we can control our emotions and say no to the fear of failure. Remember, love casts out all fear (1 John 4:18). Loving again is possible. A blended family can learn to live in their new present and embrace the future while still valuing the past. With God nothing is impossible, and by His grace you can establish a new family culture.

Family Culture

Each family has its own culture and vision, even if not developed intentionally. The daily habits and personalities of each member gradually shape the family over time. Blended families must be especially sensitive to each other since they come from different home environments. It's important to be intentional when starting to create a new family culture. For example, you will need to discuss the following:

- How will the holidays (Christmas and birthdays) be spent?
- What are the expectations for helping with chores around the house?
- What are the nighttime curfews for the teenagers?
- What types of shows are the children allowed to watch on television?
- What are the expectations for the children's personal hygiene?
- What kind of food does each family member prefer?
- What kind of vacations do the children enjoy?

These are areas that were already established in their previous home environment, but it takes intentionality and good communication to determine how they will work in the new family dynamic.

One of the most important things is to treat the children equally. Give clear communication about expectations. There cannot be "my rules for my children" and "your rules for your children." It takes the best of both worlds to establish a successful blended culture. **The keys to raising the children together are unity, equality, and clarity. We make decisions together, we treat the children equally, and we are clear about what we expect.** Sometimes there are expectations that parents assume their children will automatically understand. But it doesn't happen that way; as they say in Mexico, "Cada cabeza es un mundo diferente." ("Everyone's mind is a different world.") What is obvious to you may not be obvious to the other person, especially if you did not grow up together. Frustration over small differences is common in any family but even more so in blended families. Take the time to talk it through before you start complaining and correcting.

The children's emotional attachment to their parent's new spouse takes time, and it is more likely to happen with good communication, prayerful patience, and lots of love. The stepparent does not need to be the children's best friend (though hopefully they are not their worst enemy), but each member needs to feel comfortable in the role they have within the family structure. Find moments of connection with new activities or routines that you can develop together and embrace some of the familiar traditions of the original family. For example, perhaps the children comment that they used to enjoy going out to breakfast from time to time as a family when their dad was at home. Now that he is absent, they miss those family times. This is a good opportunity for the new stepfather to ask if they would like to continue to do that as a family or if they would like to start a new tradition with him. The children will give you clues as to where their hearts are in the process. It is so important to be sensitive to their process, rather than pressure them to be where you want them to be.

Healthy Boundaries

This point is extremely important, because God established natural limits of attraction and respect between parents, children, and siblings. This means that an emotionally and spiritually healthy man will not have a physical attraction to his adolescent daughter. He has an innate sense of protection toward her, and his love is pure and fatherly. However, not everyone is emotionally and spiritually stable, and there are cases in which these limits have been crossed even in the original families. The consequences are devastating. Sadly, the statistics of abuse are higher in blended families because there is no biological boundary between the stepfather and child. Setting guidelines from the beginning will help protect the family dynamic. This is also true for children of the opposite sex who are not biological siblings. They should not be left alone unsupervised. Sexual curiosity is normal in children, and even in biological families we must help our children manage their sexuality correctly. The probability of sexual abuse when children are not related is much higher than when children are biological siblings.

For this same reason, particularly in the beginning, use practical wisdom in the way the family interacts. Special awareness needs to be given to modesty. Also, hugs and other forms of physical affection between new members of the family should be expressed with extra care. We know of blended families who were naive about this issue and later tragically discovered sexual abuse happening within the family. In one case, the mother did not protect her child because she didn't want to believe her and put the new relationship at risk. She decided her daughter was exaggerating, so she did nothing. We can't be naive. At the first sign of someone crossing the line or the first complaint from your child, the situation should be addressed and immediate action taken.

Another important limit is in the area of stepparents applying discipline. It is best at the beginning that they have limited participation. Later, with time and earned trust, they can become more involved in disciplining the children. It is helpful to discuss it early on and reevaluate as necessary. Involving older children by talking with them about how you plan to discipline sets the environment of open communication in the home. Listen to their opinions. Remember, you are a family now, and the goal is unity.

Blended Finances

Family finances are another important topic to address. A lack of communication can lead to differences that turn into conflicts and end in a crisis. Good money management at home is essential to a successful marriage. Knowing how much money you have, how assets or debts are managed, who is responsible for what, as well as the goals of how the money is going to be spent or invested, are important in all families. They are even more critical in a blended family. Blended finances can be complicated, so total transparency is key to peace and trust in the relationship.

In Chapter 7: Money Matters, we gave a detailed explanation of how to manage resources according to the natural and spiritual laws God gives us in His Word. The same principles apply to a blended family. One difference, though, is the budget. Special attention needs to be given to what is allotted for alimony and child support. In counseling, we often see wives who resent the amount of money given in this area. This is a common reaction, but it is not correct. It is better to thank God that your husband is a responsible father who loves his children. Consider it a basic necessity in your budget (similar to the rent/mortgage and grocery bills). That money does not belong to you. You knew you were marrying a man with a former wife and children. Release the money with gratitude, like you would any offering to the Lord.

> You must each decide in your heart how much to give. And don't give reluctantly or in response to pressure. "For God loves a person who gives cheerfully." And God will generously provide all you need. Then you will always have everything you need and

plenty left over to share with others (2 Corinthians 9:7-8 NLT).

God is the God of new beginnings. ==If His original plan for our lives was shattered by our sin or by situations beyond our control, He doesn't have a plan B. All His plans become plan A. God is not the God of second chances but of new opportunities! Remember, His mercies are new every morning== (Lamentations 3:23). And His promises stand forever:

> And the God of all grace, who called you to his eternal glory in Christ, after you have suffered a little while, will himself restore you and make you strong, firm and steadfast. To him be the power for ever and ever. Amen (1 Peter 5:10-11).

GOD IS THE GOD OF RESTORATION!

Conclusion

God's divine intervention is what makes it possible for us to have a divine marriage. We can't do it on our own, and it doesn't depend on us doing everything right. God never asks us to be perfect, but He does ask us to be willing. Are we willing to do whatever it takes to better our marriage? Are we willing to humble ourselves and surrender our relationship to God? If we are, then we can take hold of the incredible promise that He "is able to do immeasurably more than all we ask or imagine, according to his power that is at work within us" (Ephesians 3:20). We have seen firsthand how our family has been transformed by the power of God as we put Matthew 6:33 into practice: "Seek the Kingdom of God above all else, and live righteously, and he will give you everything you need" (NLT). We have also seen His miraculous works in other families who have been willing to walk the restoration process with Him.

We hope we have encouraged and inspired you to seek the Lord for a divine marriage. If you want to invite Jesus to take control of your life, simply receive what He already did for you on the cross. Today is an excellent day to rededicate your marriage to God, surrendering your family to His care. We leave you with this prayer that we encourage you to pray together with your spouse:

> Lord Jesus, we thank You for the opportunity to know You and belong to Your Kingdom. Today we decide to make You the Lord and Savior of our marriage. We give You everything we are and everything we have. We put our future in Your hands. We believe that You are the Son of God and that You came to rescue us and not condemn us. We ask for Your forgiveness for our faults and sins. We want our marriage and family to represent Your Kingdom here on earth. Holy Spirit, we invite You to dwell within our hearts, and we ask You to help us and guide us to know how to use the authority we have in Christ Jesus. We resist all demonic influence, oppression, affliction, and disease from our lives. And we declare that we are more than conquerors because of the blood of Jesus and the power of our testimony. We receive our heavenly Father's blessing and all of Your promises that You have already prepared for those who love You. Thank You, God, for this opportunity to realign our lives with Your will. We decide today to walk in faith, making You the center of our divine marriage. In Jesus' name, Amen!

Made in the USA
Columbia, SC
29 December 2023